100% UNOFFICIAL

VALORANT

ESSENTIAL FIELD GUIDE

100%
UNOFFICIAL

First published in Great Britain in 2021 by 100% Unofficial,
a part of Farshore.

An imprint of HarperCollins*Publishers*
1 London Bridge Street, London SE1 9GF
www.farshore.co.uk

HarperCollins*Publishers*
1st Floor, Watermarque Building, Ringsend Road
Dublin 4, Ireland

Written by Daniel Lipscombe
Edited by Craig Jelley
Designed by Joe Bolder
Flag images used under license from Shutterstock.com

This book is an original creation by Farshore

ISBN 978 0 7555 0269 1
Printed in Italy
001

A CIP catalogue record for this title is available from the British Library.

ONLINE SAFETY FOR YOUNGER FANS

Spending time online is great fun! Here are a few simple rules to help younger fans stay safe and keep the internet a great place to spend time.

- Never give out your real name – don't use it as your username.
- Never give out any of your personal details.
- Never tell anybody which school you go to or how old you are.
- Never tell anybody your password, except a parent or guardian.
- Be aware that you must be 13 or over to create an account on many sites. Always check the site policy and ask a parent or guardian for permission before registering.
- Always tell a parent or guardian if something is worrying you.

Stay safe online. Any website addresses listed in this book are correct at the time of going to print. However, Farshore is not responsible for content hosted by third parties. Please be aware that online content can be subject to change and websites can contain content that is unsuitable for children. We advise that all children are supervised when using the internet.

Farshore takes its responsibility to the planet and its inhabitants very seriously. We aim to use papers from well-managed forests run by responsible suppliers.

100% UNOFFICIAL

VALORANT

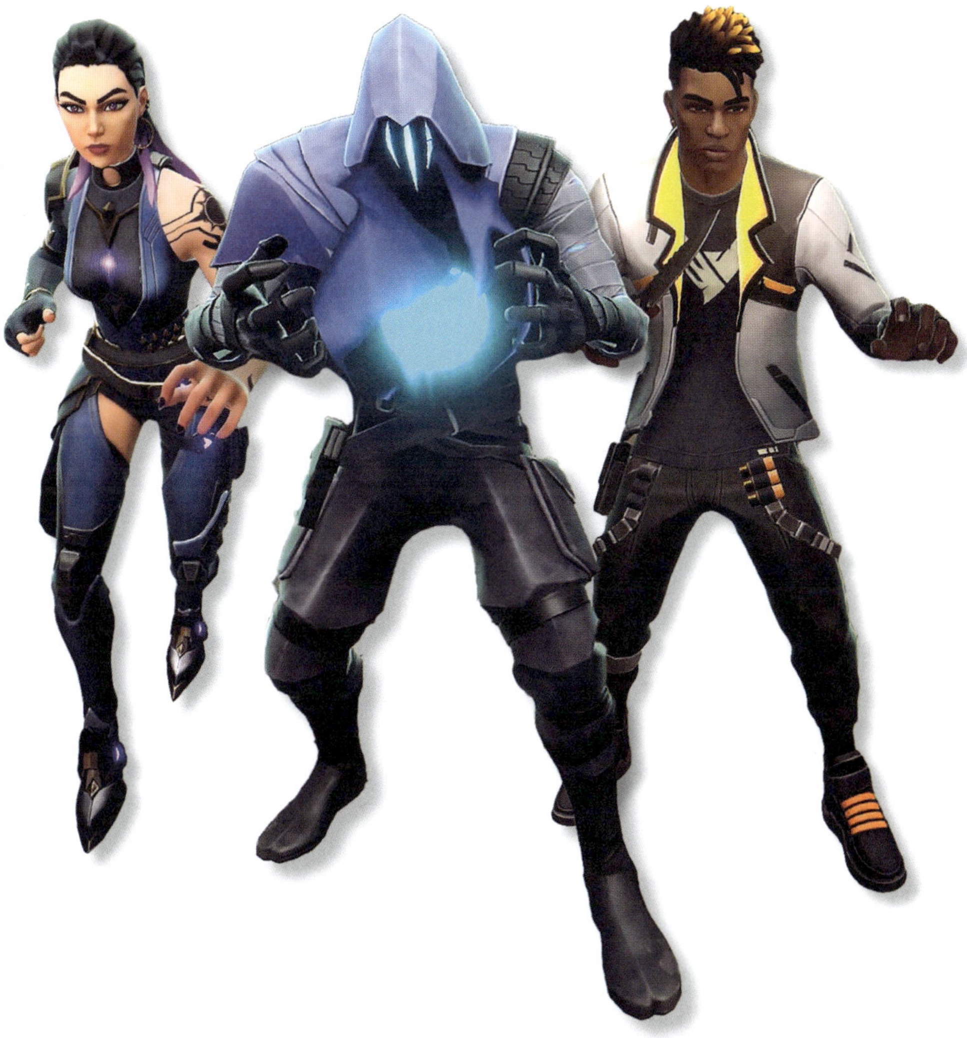

ESSENTIAL FIELD GUIDE

CONTENTS

Hello Agent,

Welcome to the near future - a world in turmoil, after an event known as The First Light transformed technology, politics and life itself. Following the days of The First Light, shady organisations crept out from the darkness to harness the power awakened in members of the public.

Agents from around the world were brought together under the Valorant Protocol - some use their newfound powers for good, others want to wreak havoc and destruction. It's up to you and your team to take control and fight for the future of this timeline.

You're tasked with stopping opposing agents via tactical missions that require skilled gunplay, mastery of special abilities and teamwork to secure victory. You will travel the Earth across several maps, visiting the futuristic Middle East, the slums of South America, as well as the pagodas and mountains of the Far East and the ruins of Europe.

Whichever path you choose, you have much to learn.
Get yourself prepped and ready, it's time to fight.

Welcome to Valorant.

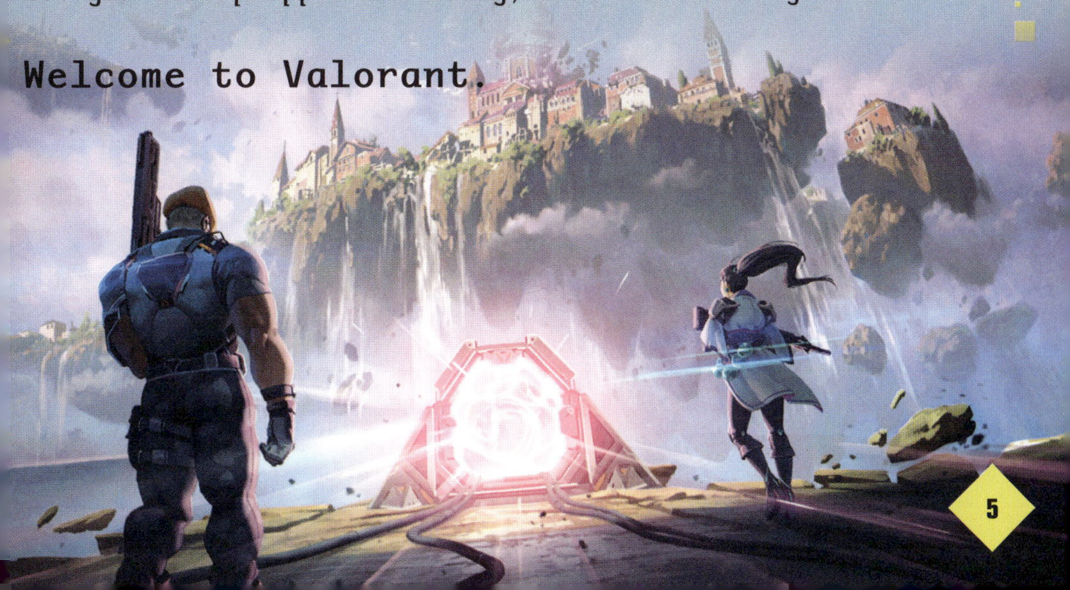

VALORANT EXPLAINED

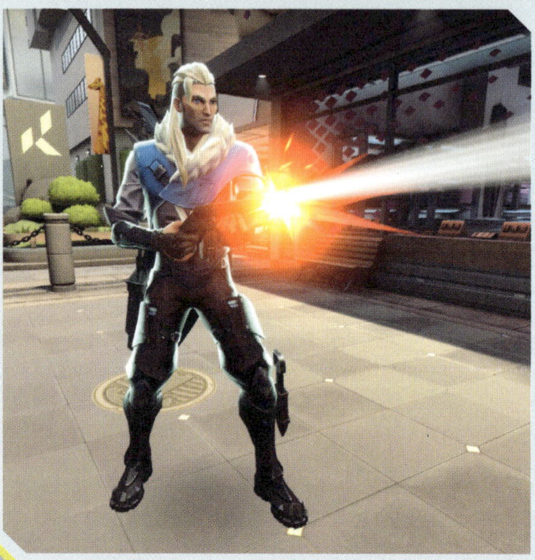

GAMEPLAY

Valorant is a highly tactical shooter that relies heavily on teamwork and balancing weapon skill with unique abilities. In the standard modes, two teams war against each other, taking turns to attack and defend. The attacking team must plant a 'spike' in the opposing team's half of the map, while the defenders try to stop them by either wiping out the team or defusing the planted 'spike'.

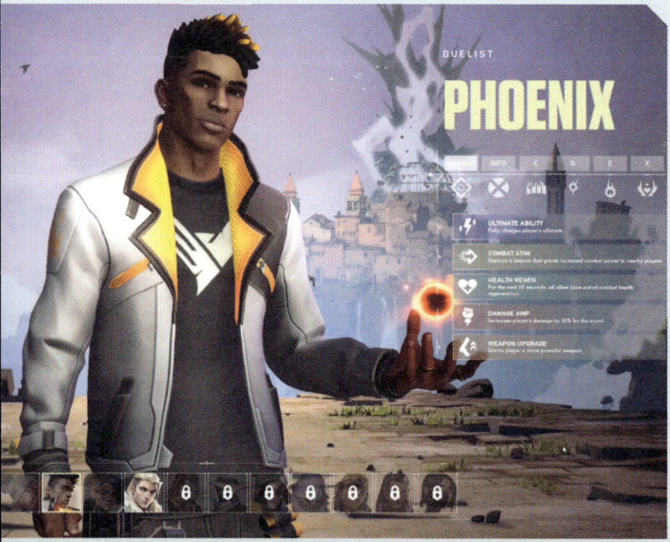

AGENTS

Teams are comprised of 'agents', of which there are 13 to choose from. No agent can be featured twice on a team, and teams should try to balance more defensive agents with those of a greater attacking capability. Each agent has a different class that establishes how they're best used, which is determined by the skills they have at their disposal.

WEAPONS

The arsenal is bursting with genre staples. There are precise snipers, rapid machine guns, versatile assault rifles and deadly shotguns. Much like the agents, there's a weapon to suit every playstyle – if you prefer to get into the action you'll find close-quarters weapons most attractive, whereas patient players can equip a sniper rifle, hang back on the maps and dominate the enemy team from afar.

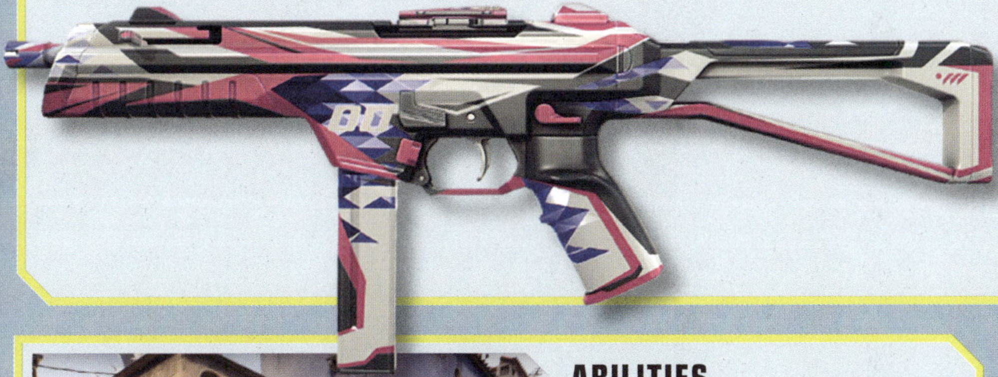

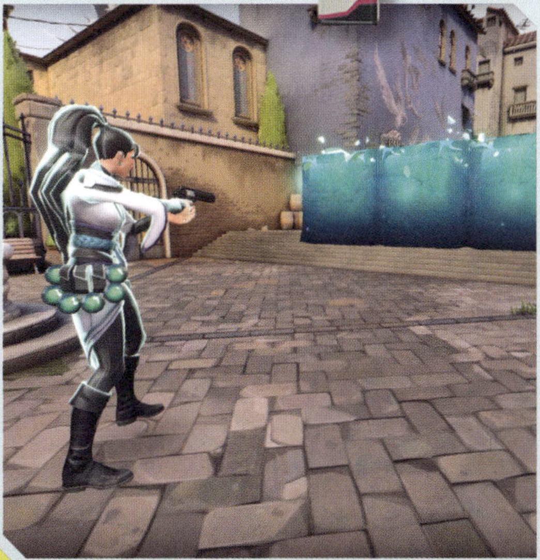

ABILITIES

These agents are masters of the mystical powers of 'The First Light'. Some use their powers for good, others ... not so much. But whichever side your favourite falls on, they have powerful abilities at their fingertips, from smoke bombs to walls of poisonous gas. Some agents are all about damage output and their abilities reflect that, while others want to stop the enemy dead in their tracks by creating walls or covering the floor in flames.

AGENTS

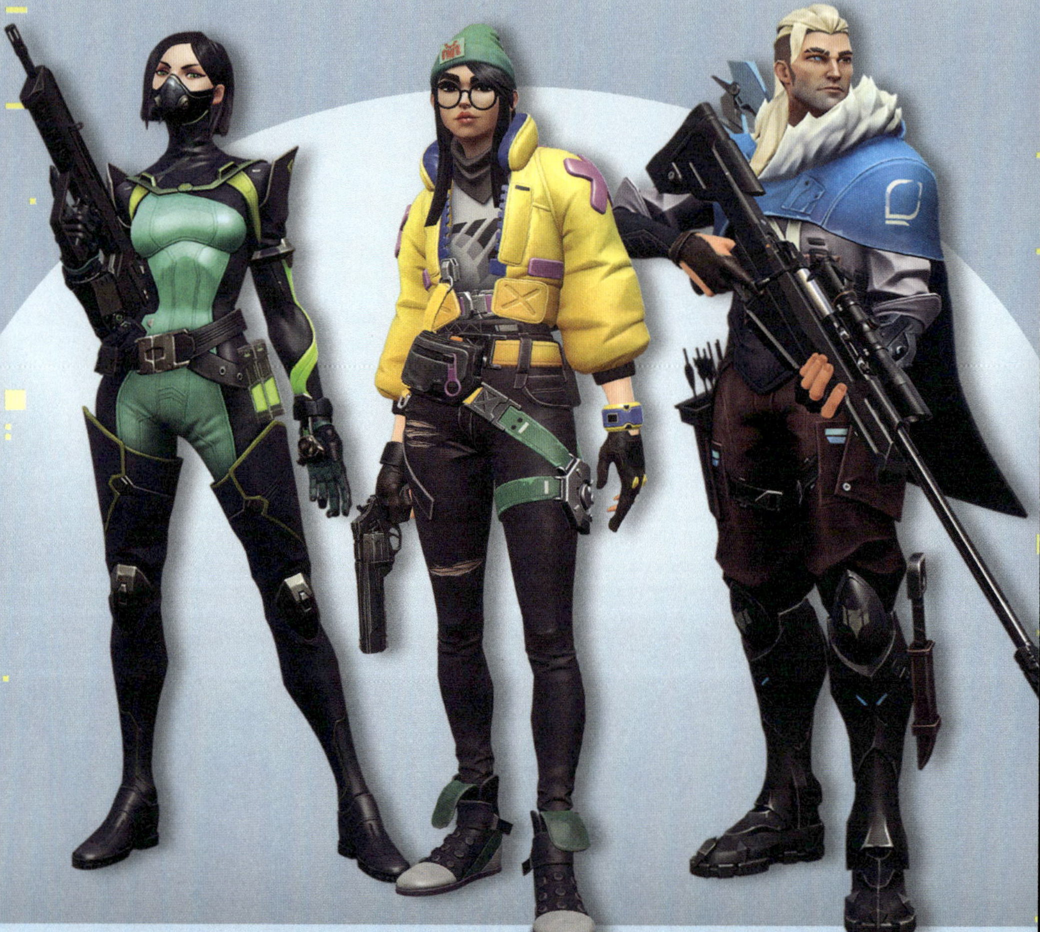

When you first start out, there will be five agents available for you to use. In order to unlock the rest of the roster, you must earn XP from playing games to get agent tokens from the battle pass, which will allow you to unlock the next two agents. After this, you will need to complete Agent Contracts which are activated in the 'Collection' tab. Once you have selected the agent you want to unlock and have activated their contract, simply reach level five of the contract and they're all yours to play with.

CLASSES

Each of the agents play very differently to one another, but each fall within one of four classes. Think about how you naturally play shooting games and which agent would suit your playstyle in this kind of game.

DUELIST

These are your main attackers; their abilities bolster their threat when pushing into a fight. They're often a lot stronger in battle but rarely offer their team support.

INITIATOR

Initiators gather information about where the enemy team is positioned across areas of the map or have skills that let them initiate pushes into enemy territory.

SENTINEL

This class can usually be found at the back of the battle, lending support to the frontline fighters. They can often heal or even revive a teammate after they've died.

CONTROLLER

Controllers offer ways to block off an enemy push by creating walls or blocking line-of-sight, preventing the enemy from being able to aim at you or your teammates.

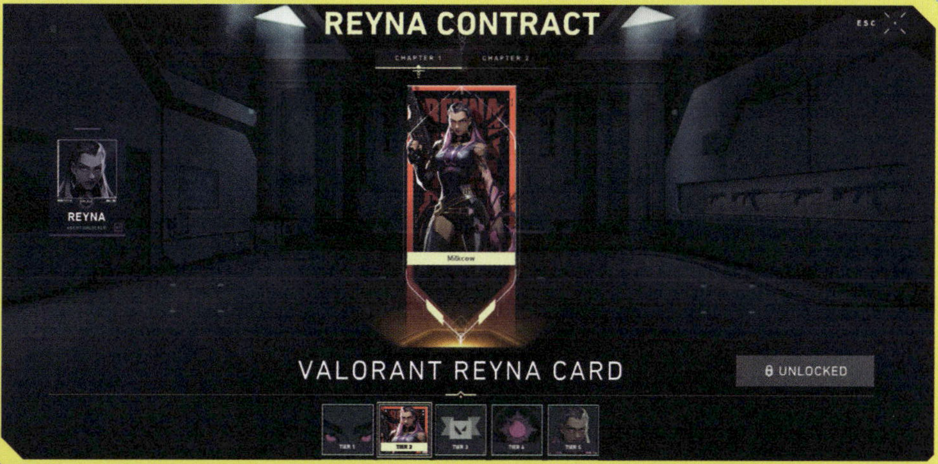

BREACH

// INITIATOR

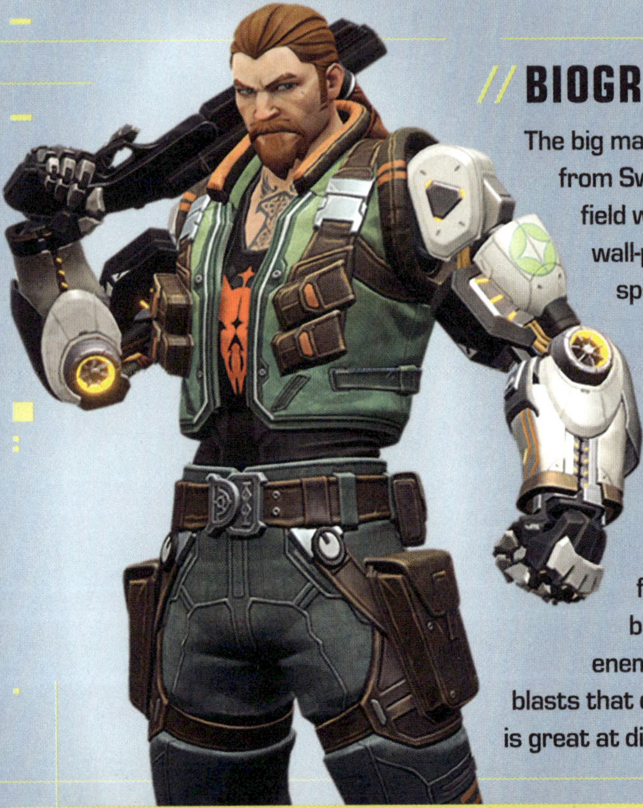

// BIOGRAPHY

The big man with the bionic arms hails from Sweden. He divides the playing field with huge kinetic blasts and wall-piercing barrages. As the spearhead of a team, Breach can clear a path to enemy turf and guide his team to victory.

All of his skills can penetrate through map structures, allowing him to blind and deal damage from behind cover. Between blinding balls of light that disable enemies and earth-shattering blasts that dizzy everyone in range, Breach is great at disorienting foes for a rush entry.

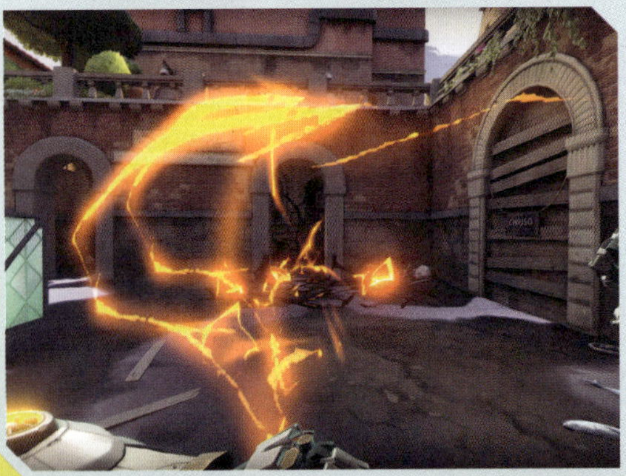

FAULT LINE

Breach's signature skill causes seismic blasts to tear through the ground towards the enemy. This can be used through walls in a chosen area of effect and disorients those who feel the shock. With an adjustable range, it can be used as a quick burst or to shake foes far away.

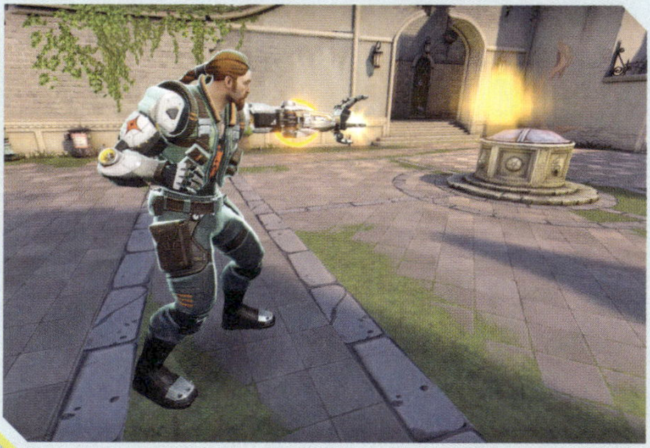

FLASHPOINT

Contorting his left bionic hand, Breach generates a bright ball of light that shoots through walls, blinding anyone on the other side who happens to see it. It's handy for getting a team onto a plant site while enemies are out of action.

AFTERSHOCK

Breach's right hand can also transform – into a cannon. It conjures a cylinder of light in the air, which turns into a nasty fireball as it erupts through walls, dealing damage to anyone in its path. Perfect for clearing out tight corridors or driving out hiding enemies.

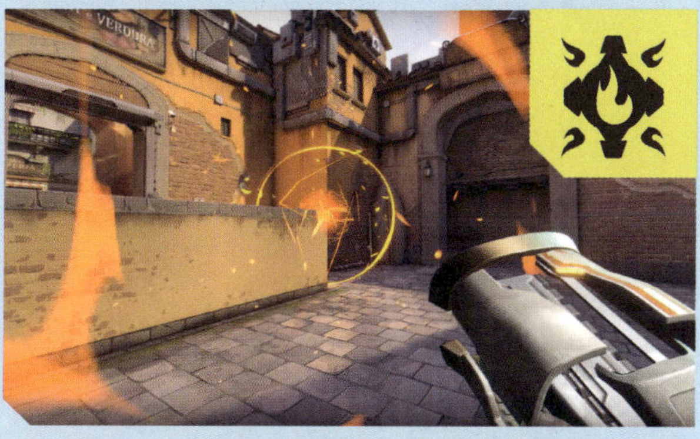

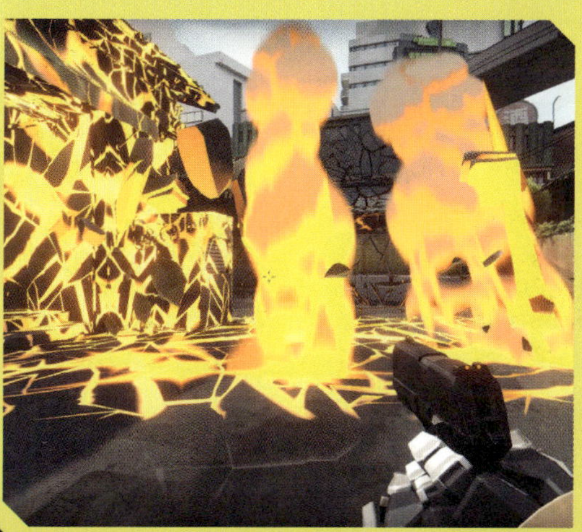

ROLLING THUNDER

For Breach's ultimate ability, he combines the power in both arms to send a cascading wave of destruction hurtling towards the enemy. The ground tears apart, crumbling and sending chunks of concrete flying. Anyone caught in the blast is blown backwards and seriously dazed, unable to think or fire straight. A well-aimed blast can bring a team to their knees as they try to plant the spike.

BRIMSTONE

// CONTROLLER

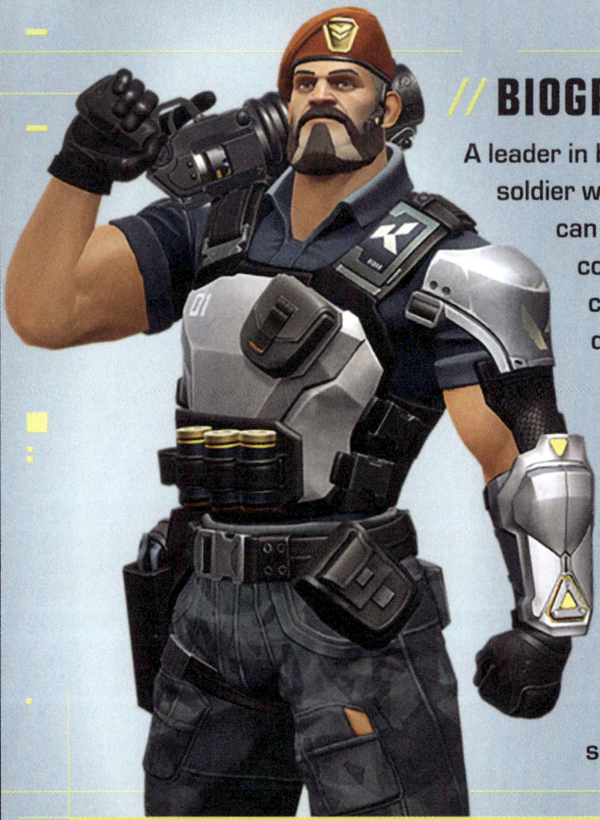

// BIOGRAPHY

A leader in battle, Brimstone is a no-nonsense soldier who commands an aerial fleet that can lend the team distractions or cover as necessary. He also has a couple of portable gadgets he can deploy himself.

Brim's abilities make him a good starting agent. His skills are versatile enough that he can hold sites with smokes and path-blocking fire, or push forward, masking lines of sight and boosting teammates speed. He likes to control the map, funnelling enemies into tight situations where he lies in wait.

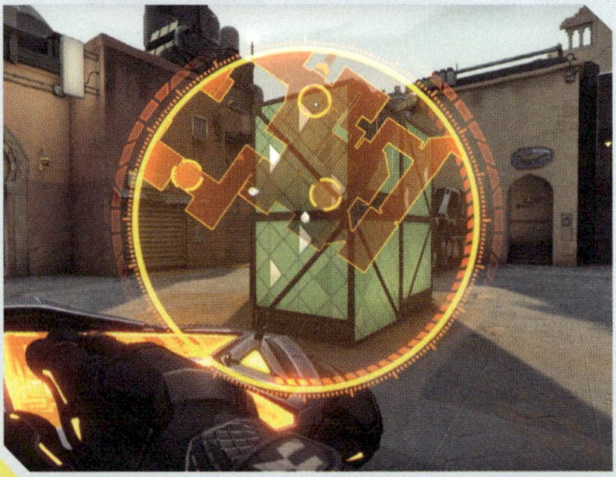

SKY SMOKE

Calling up a tactical map of the immediate area, Brimstone can make smoke grenades fall from the heavens on up to three locations. Upon landing, these grenades burst into a dome of covering smoke shielding his team from view or obscuring the sight lines of the opposing team.

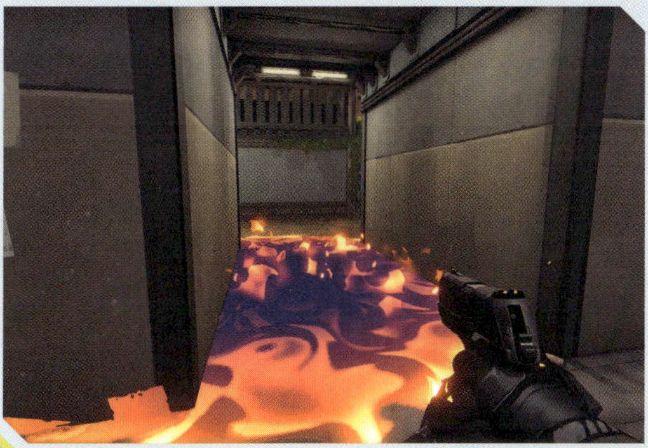

INCENDIARY

Pulling out a grenade launcher, Brimstone fires a canister of liquid fire to blanket an area, damaging anyone who walks through it. This skill is ideal for holding choke points or firing through windows to flush out a camping sniper.

STIM BEACON

If Brimstone or his teammates need more firepower, this handy stim beacon can be thrown onto the floor, creating a radius of effect. Anyone standing within the zone will find their weapon has an increased rate of fire, allowing them to launch a hail of bullets towards the unsuspecting enemy.

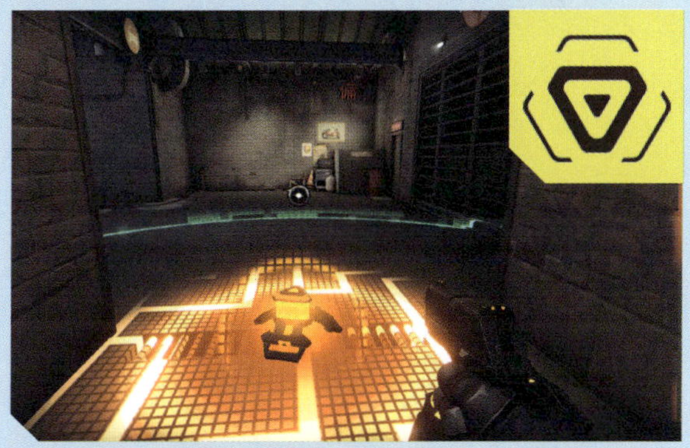

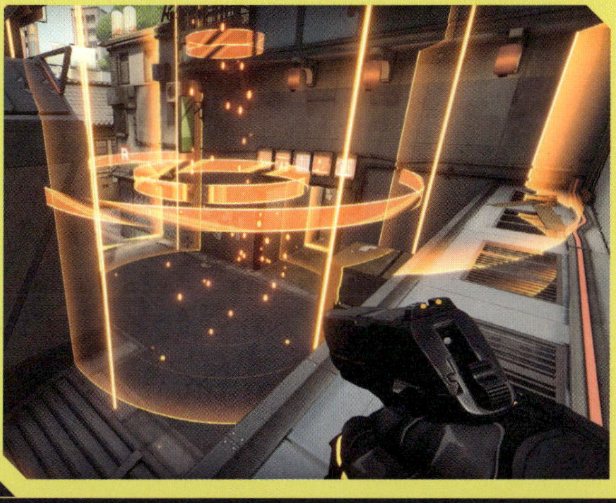

ORBITAL STRIKE

Going back to his tactical map, Brimstone gathers the full power of his circling fleet and calls in an aerial blitz on a chosen location. Once called, there's no going back and his enemies will be decimated by a cannon of lingering, laser-guided hellfire. It can also damage allies too, so be wary.

CYPHER

// SENTINEL

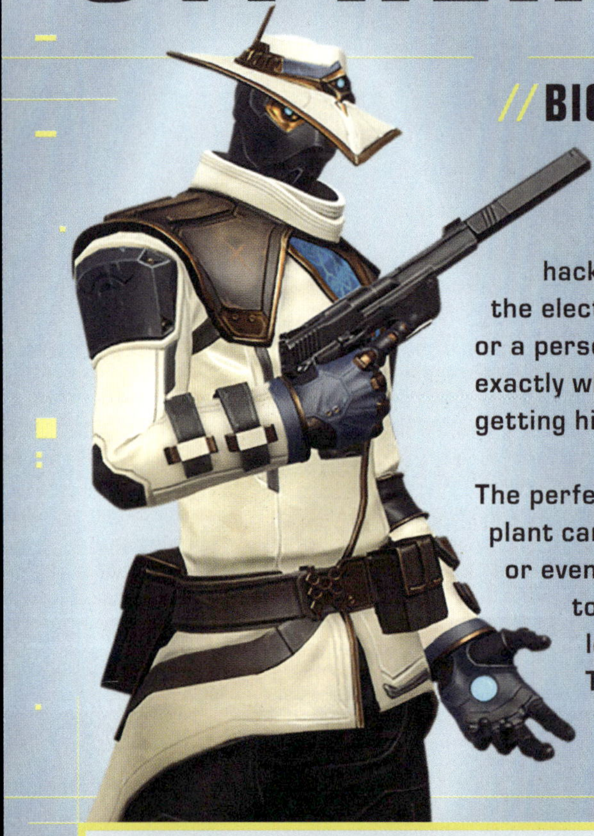

// BIOGRAPHY

Cypher watches everything and everyone. He's a one-man surveillance network, able to hack into any connection, whether the electronics dwell inside a building, or a person. He prides himself on knowing exactly what's going on at all times, only getting his hands dirty when needs must.

The perfect support agent, Cypher can plant cameras to watch over areas, or even hack into defeated enemies to relay information of enemy locations to his teammates. This man of mystery is ideal for dropping behind enemy lines or setting up the perfect trap.

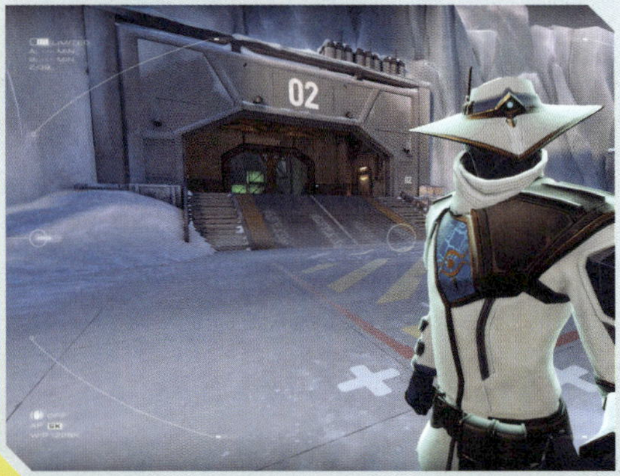

SPYCAM

Cypher's main ability allows him to fire a small spycam onto any surface. When the ability is activated again, he can watch from the camera and pass info to his team, or fire a tracking dart into a passing player. This removable dart then briefly displays that enemy's position to everyone in Cypher's team.

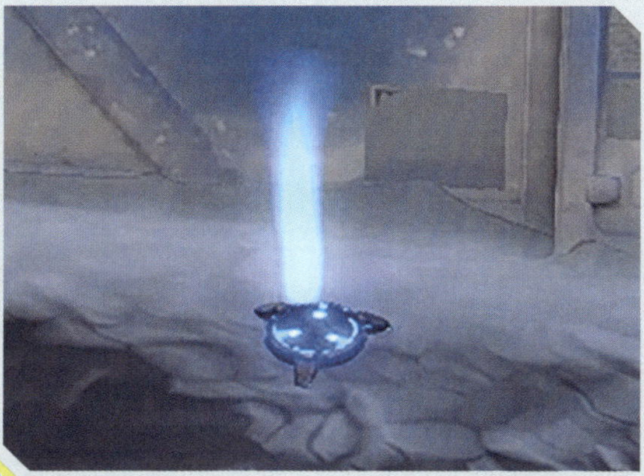

CYBER CAGE

Cypher can lob a device on the floor, and trigger it from a distance to raise a cage. Not only does this completely block enemy vision, but if they try to walk through to see what's on the other side, there will be an audible trigger, and the enemy will be slowed down too.

TRAPWIRE

This places a tripwire between two points on a map. If an enemy trips through the beam, it will show their location and completely daze them if they don't destroy the mechanism quickly. If Cypher changes his mind on placement, the trapwire can be easily removed and placed elsewhere.

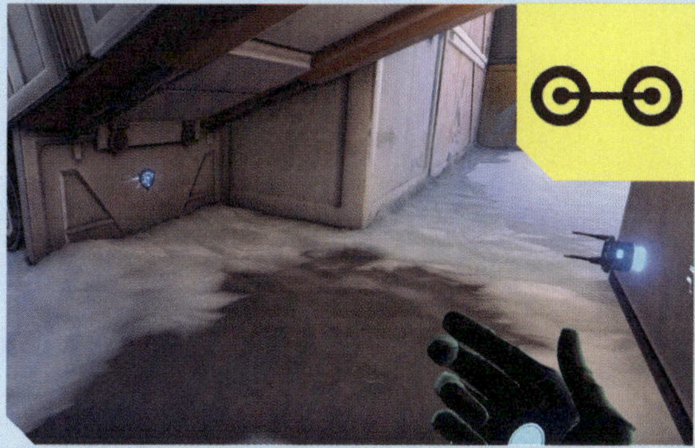

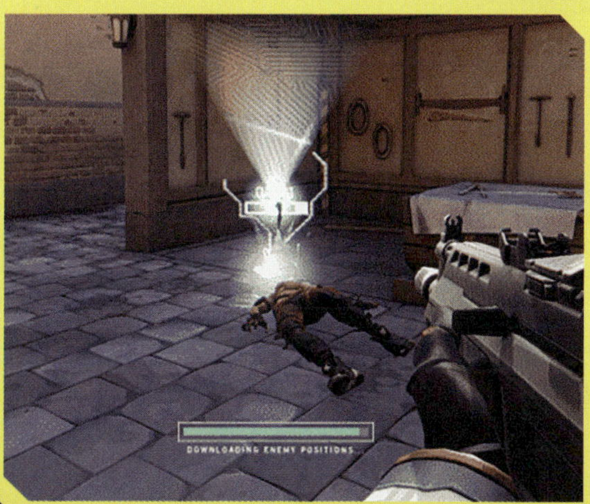

NEURAL THEFT

Throwing his high-tech hat over a defeated enemy, Cypher takes over the last fragments of their dying mind. He taps into their neural pathways to discover where the enemy team is hiding and reveals the information to his allies via the minimap. Unfortunately it means he has to go hat-less for the rest of the round as well.

JETT

// DUELIST

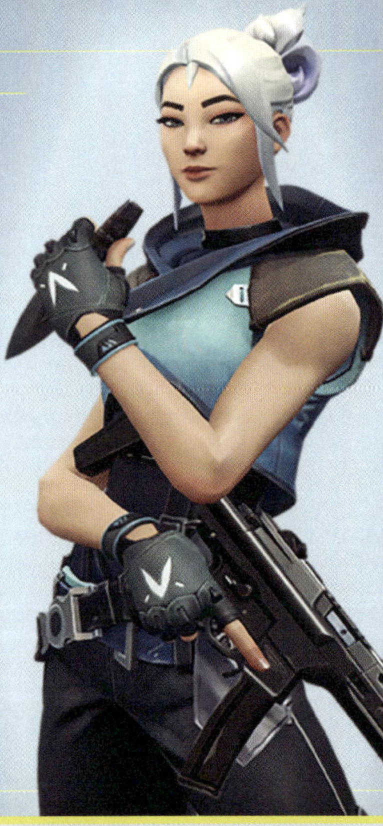

// BIOGRAPHY

Jett is a master of movement and agility. Never standing in one spot for too long, she moves like the wind to gust around the map, keeping the enemy on their toes.

She's a master of fluid movement. Whether she's dashing forward or launching herself up to high ledges, it feels like she never comes to rest. Combined with her lethal ultimate ability – which puts five wind-commanded blades at her disposal – she's a force of nature. She's also the only agent who has a passive skill: when she leaps from a height, she can press the jump key to float down, negating any potential fall damage and allowing her to aim steady.

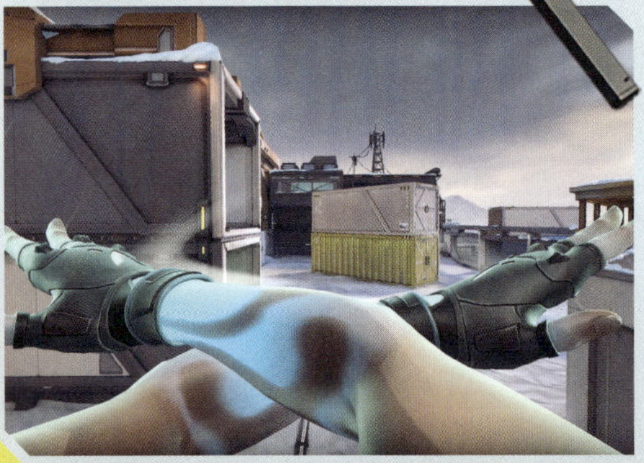

TAILWIND

With Jett's signature ability, she summons a gust of air to push her in whichever direction she's facing. This is great for moving towards an area, beating the enemy to defensive ground or dashing out of a fight to reposition or back-up a teammate.

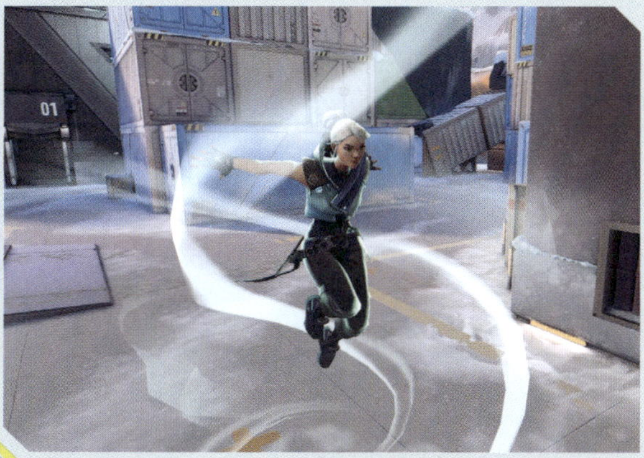

UPDRAFT

Much like Tailwind, this ability uses a blast of air. Though this time the push comes from below and sends Jett flying into the air, allowing her to reach high ledges so she can hide, or set herself up with a good vantage point to snipe from.

CLOUDBURST

The cloudburst is a guidable projectile which bursts into a dense section of cloud, blocking enemy view. This can be fired in a straight line or curved by moving the crosshair in any direction while holding the ability.

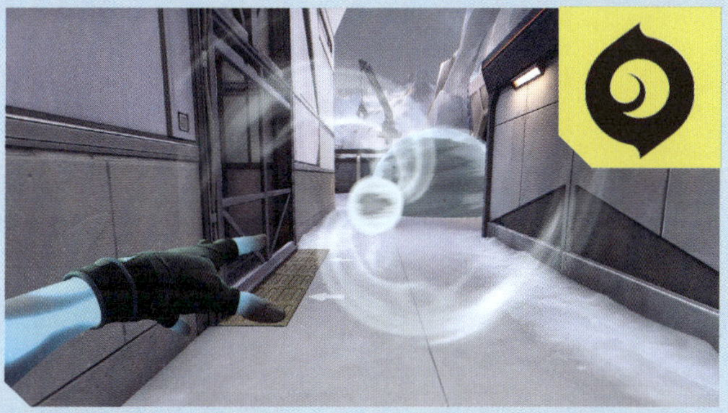

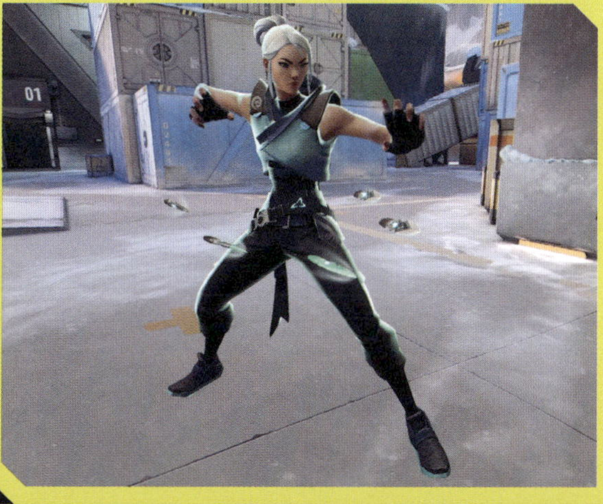

BLADE STORM

Jett calls up a storm of deadly knives, levitated by her wind powers as she moves. She can launch them one by one, or by using Alternate Fire, she can cast them all towards a single opponent shredding them where they stand. If she kills an enemy with this skill, the knives replenish, making it a deadly, reusable ultimate.

KILLJOY // SENTINEL

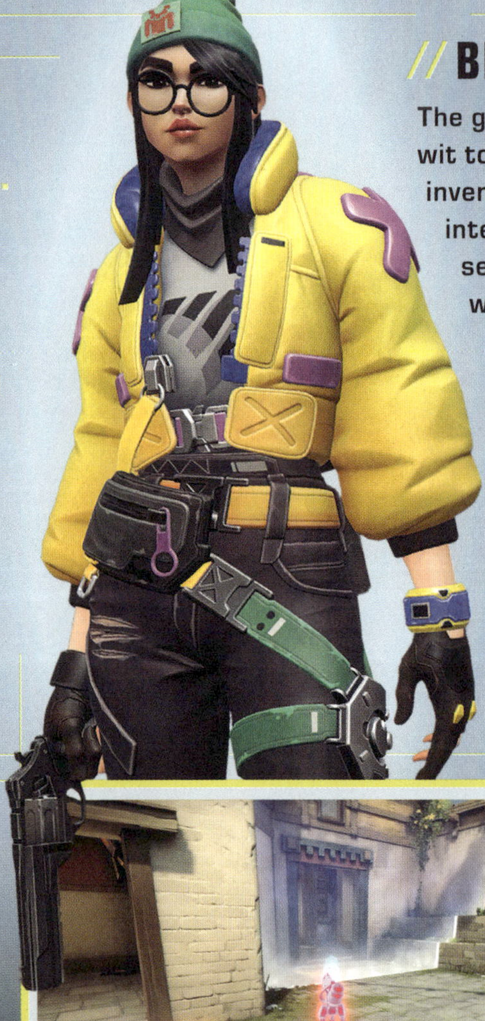

// BIOGRAPHY

The genius of Germany, Killjoy brings a dry wit to the battlefield along with her quirky inventions. While she may be incredibly intelligent, she doesn't take life too seriously and loves to have a bit of fun while fighting.

Using her homemade arsenal of weapons and gadgets, Killjoy's abilities focus on debuffing enemies and generally inconveniencing them. She straddles a fine line between defensive support character and wily attacker when her gadgets are activated, though they all have the element of surprise in common.

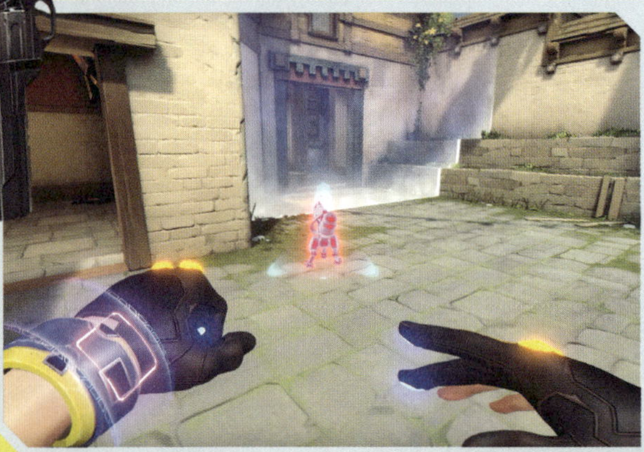

TURRET

Killjoy's primary ability allows her to place a small turret, which fires at any enemy that wanders into its cone of vision. Able to survey a 180-degree angle, this turret – if placed in the right spot – can cause plenty of mischief.

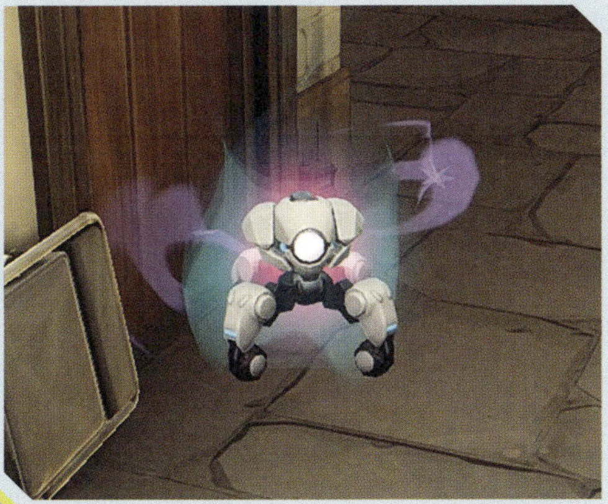

ALARMBOT

Another of Killjoy's cute creations is the alarmbot, who lies hidden in wait for an unsuspecting enemy. If one passes by, it will scuttle towards them, promptly explode and cause the vulnerable effect, which makes them less resilient to incoming damage. It also emits a sound and a visual on the minimap so allies will have a sense of where at least one enemy is.

NANOSWARM

Killjoy can throw a grenade that lies dormant and almost undetectable. She can trigger it from a distance, at which point it explodes into a swarm of tiny robots, applying a small amount of damage for a sustained period of time. Handy for protecting a planted spike.

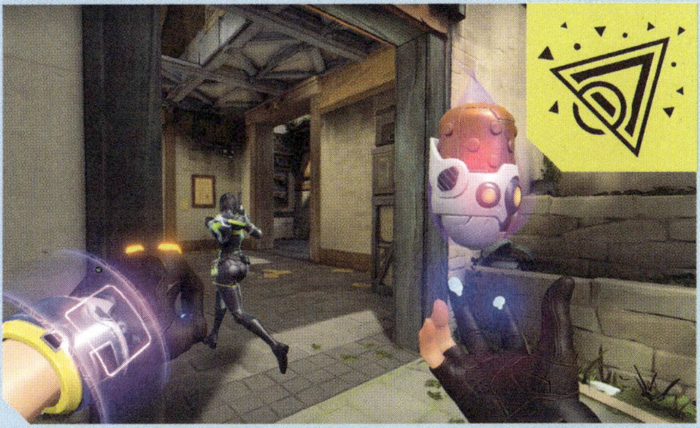

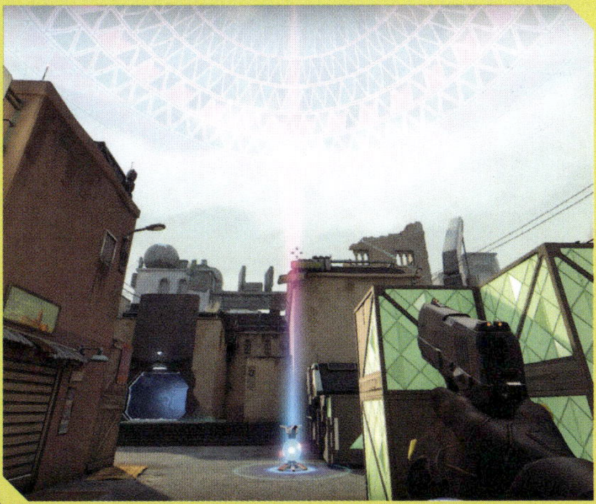

LOCKDOWN

The Lockdown device makes eliminating targets super-easy! Once planted in the ground, much like the spike, the device explodes into a wave of light trapping any enemies within its bubble after around 15 seconds has elapsed. Anyone caught is immediately slowed and unable to attack, leaving your team to dash away with the spike, or run in for the kill.

?

OMEN

// CONTROLLER

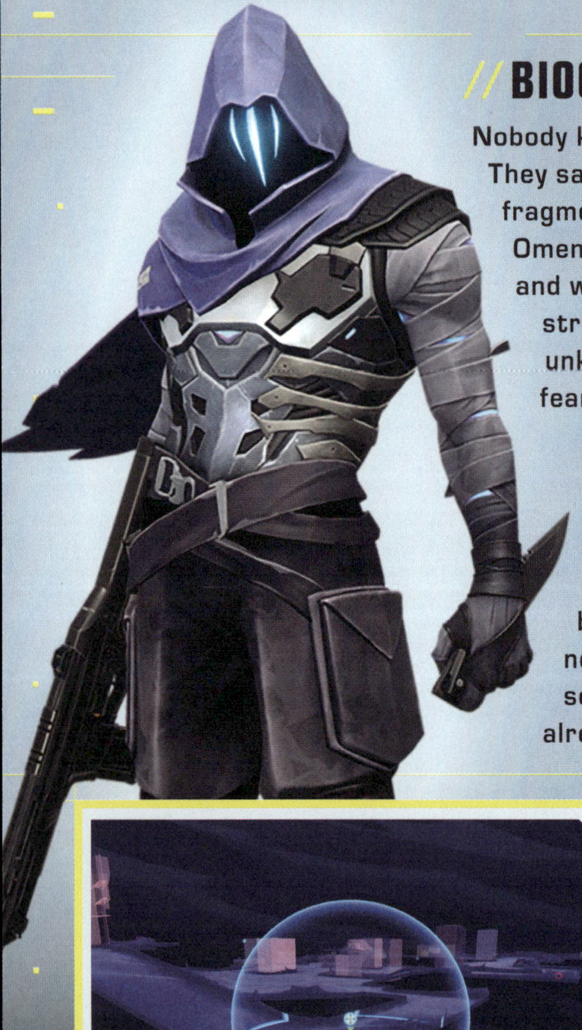

// BIOGRAPHY

Nobody knows anything about Omen. They say he is a complete mystery, a fragment of a memory; a phantom. Omen lurks in the shadows, watching and waiting, for the perfect time to strike. Channelling the power of an unknown darkness, he can spread fear throughout an enemy team.

If Omen isn't blocking enemy vision, he is sinking into the shadows, only to reappear elsewhere, either to gain a better vantage or to spring up nearer to his objective. If an enemy sees Omen on the battlefield, it's already too late for them.

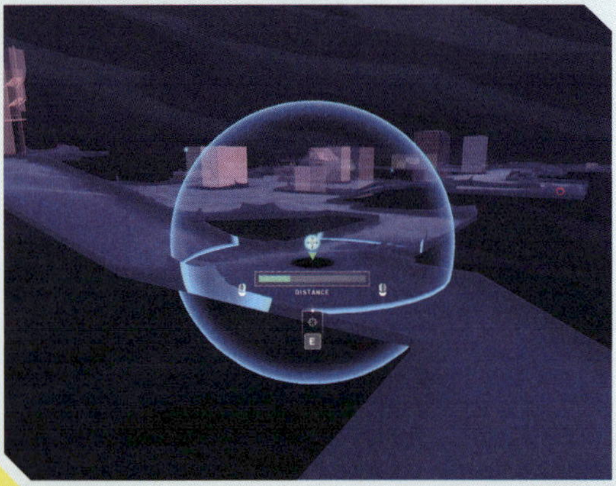

DARK COVER

Using this ability, Omen looks through the shadow dimension, where he can bypass walls and other blockages, to place an orb of smoke. While blocking the enemy's sight, Omen or his team can sneak in and take their foe by surprise. Use the reload key to swap to a real-world view.

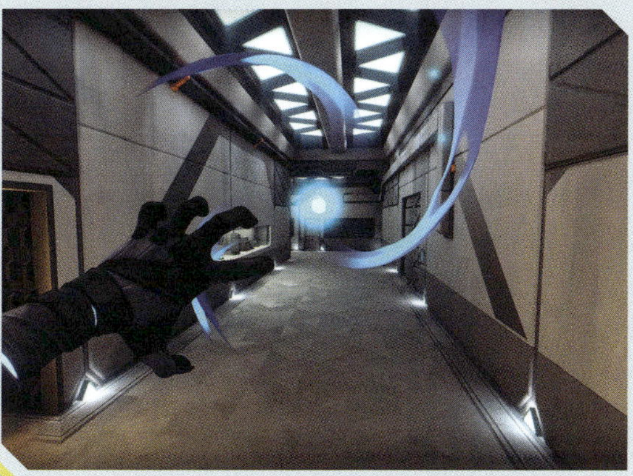

PARANOIA

This projectile attack speeds through the map in a straight line, passing through walls and enemies alike. Any enemy it touches suffers from paranoia – an engulfing shadow, which is briefly unshakable and stops them seeing anyone coming for them.

SHROUDED STEP

Conjuring a column of smoke, Omen guides the shape around, choosing the ideal place to teleport. It's great for covertly moving behind players or up to high ledges so he can watch over the battlefield, taking aim at those who walk through unawares.

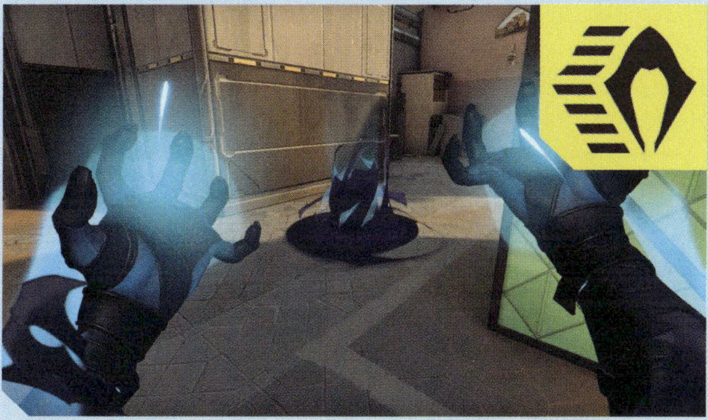

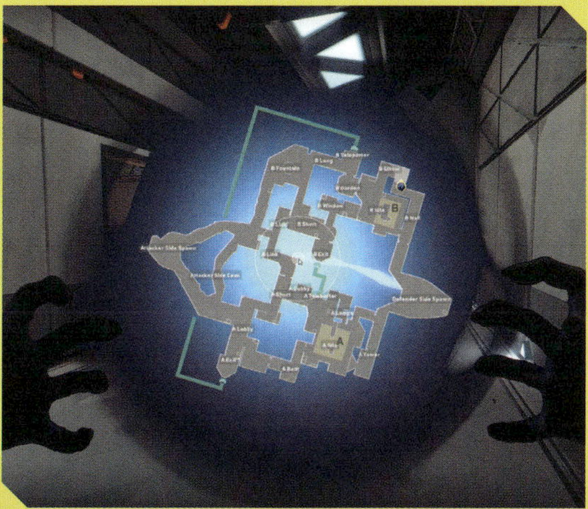

FROM THE SHADOWS

Bringing up a tactical screen, Omen chooses to teleport to any point on the map. For the first few seconds, as he transforms into smoky shadows, the teleport can be halted with damage from enemy combatants, but once the darkness takes over, he could be anywhere, armed and ever dangerous. Unlike other teleports, it has no range limit.

PHOENIX

// DUELIST

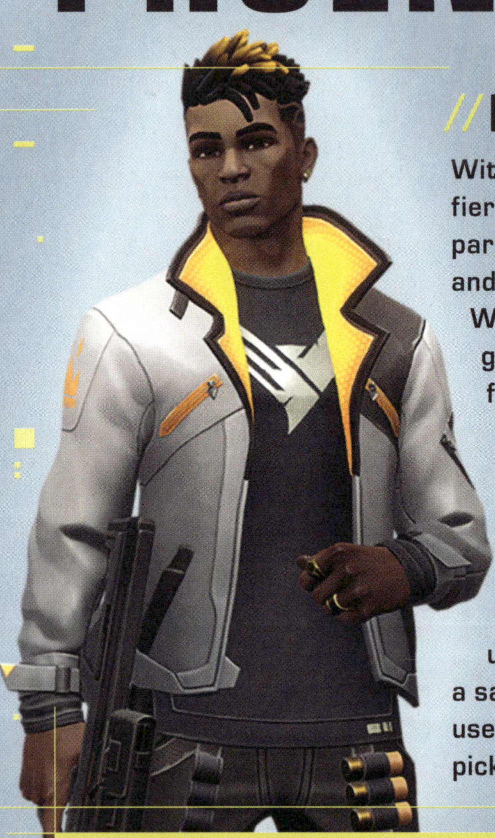

// BIOGRAPHY

With fire at his fingertips, Phoenix is a fierce warrior on the battlefield. This particular pyromancer hails from England, and controls the battlefield with a flare. Whether he rolls with his teammates or goes it alone, Phoenix is a fiery fragging force to fear.

He has a great combination of skills that can block off routes or cause significant damage, stun opponents or heal himself – he can even send an expendable decoy into the fray to unleash carnage before reanimating in a safe location. With such a wide array of useful abilities, he's a great all-rounder to pick for battle.

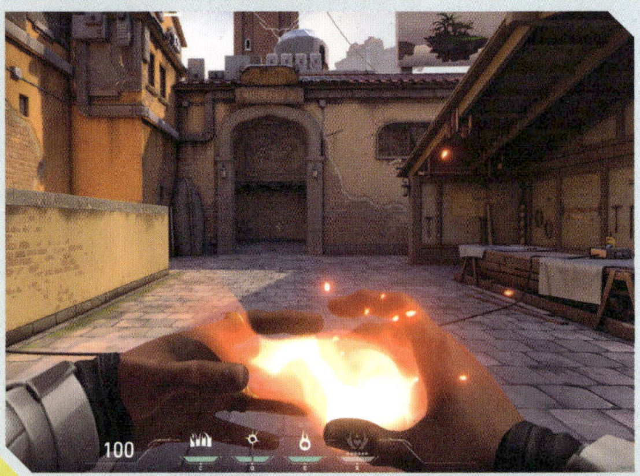

HOT HANDS

Phoenix's main skill summons a fireball to his hands, which can be launched at opponents for direct damage, lobbed into choke points to block passage, or even placed underneath Phoenix's feet, where he'll be able to draw on the inferno to restore some health.

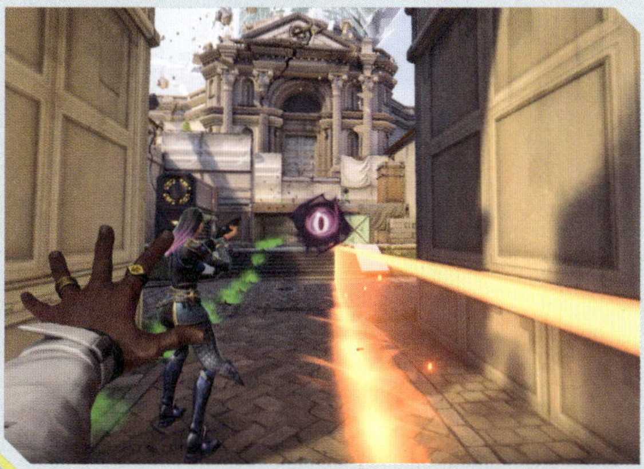

BLAZE

This ability summons a tall wall of flames that can split a route in two, either to narrow angles or block sight. The opposing team can pass through, but will take a small amount of damage. Conversely, Phoenix will heal as he passes through the flames.

CURVEBALL

Phoenix can lob a bright ember around a corner, blinding enemies that are camping an area and giving your team a window to push and open fire. Be careful not to blind yourself though or the advantage is wasted. You can use the Fire and Alternate Fire keys to throw in different directions.

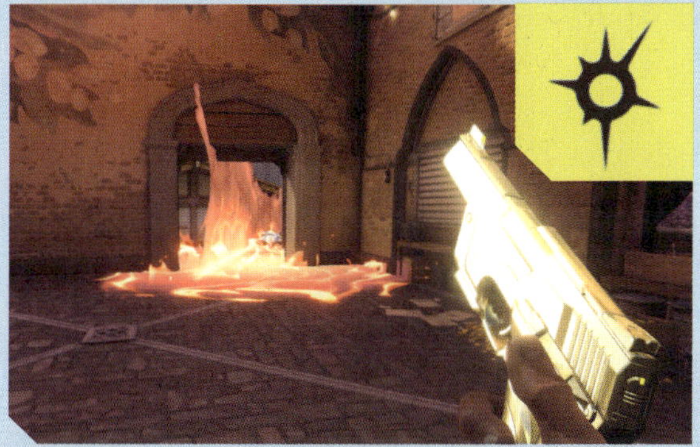

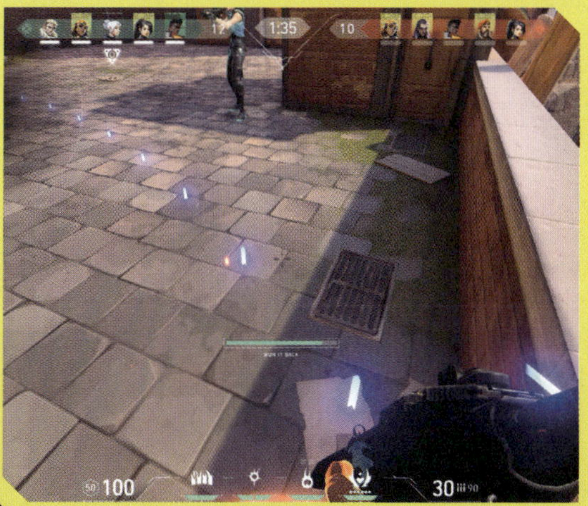

RUN THAT BACK

Wait until you're in a safe, covered spot to use Phoenix's ultimate. You'll pin your position in time and send a clone out for a short period of time to do the dirty work. You can still be killed in this form, but when you die, you'll ping back to the spot where you started the ability. It's great for doing recon and thinning out the enemy squad before you go again.

RAZE

// DUELIST

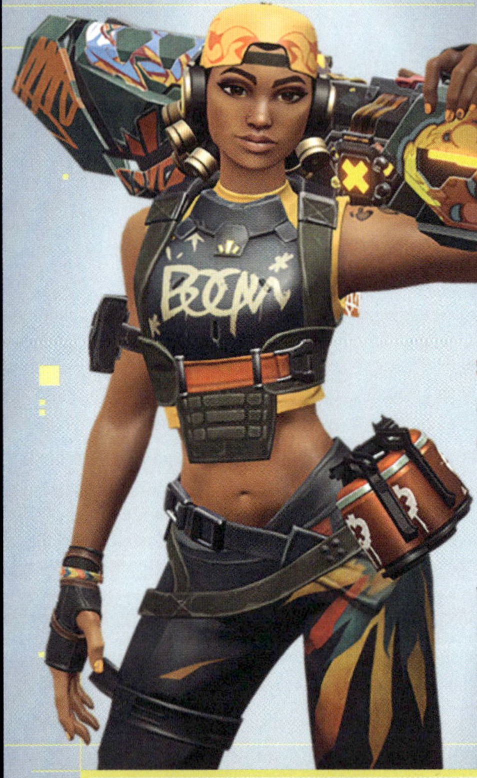

// BIOGRAPHY

Raze always enters the battlefield with a boom! Her explosive style is all about shock and awe, with bombastic touches of flair. She flourishes with her spray paint cans and trundling bots, leaking personality everywhere she goes.

Whether she's sending out her robot helper to explosively chase an enemy or wielding a rocket launcher to close out a round, she's an aggressive force to be reckoned with. Her blast packs give her an unpredictable movement style too.

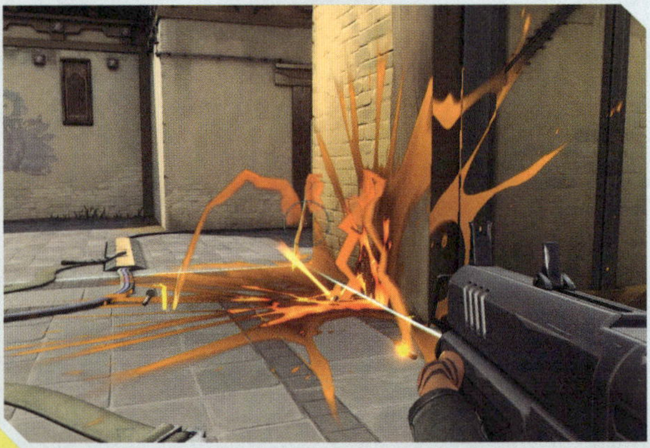

PAINT SHELLS

Raze's paint shells act like a cluster grenade, as it lands it bursts into smaller explosions, painting the area with a special concoction. It damages enemies close to the blast, plus makes everything look lovely and colourful!

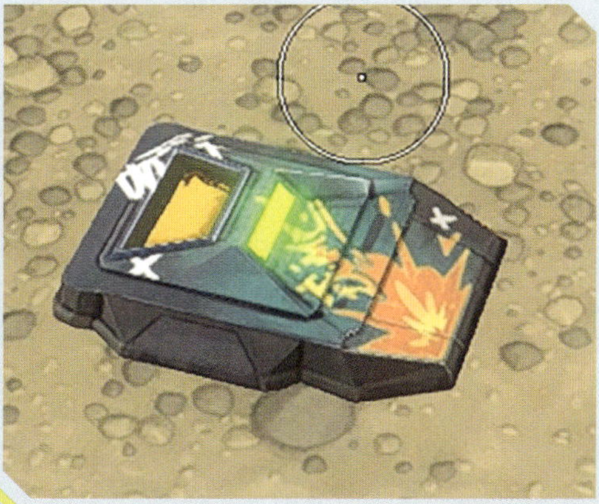

BLAST PACK

Throwing a blast pack causes damage in the vicinity as it explodes outwards, sending agents flying in random directions. This sticky pack can be thrown on walls, floors, ceilings, even onto the enemy themselves. Raze can also use it to blast herself in whichever direction she is moving – great for fast movement or reaching high spots.

BOOM BOT

The Boom Bot gives a little smile before it sets out on the trail of destruction. The adorable smile and waddling movement hide the havoc it can wreak as it seeks out enemies in the area, bouncing off walls until it finally blows up, hopefully eliminating an enemy with it.

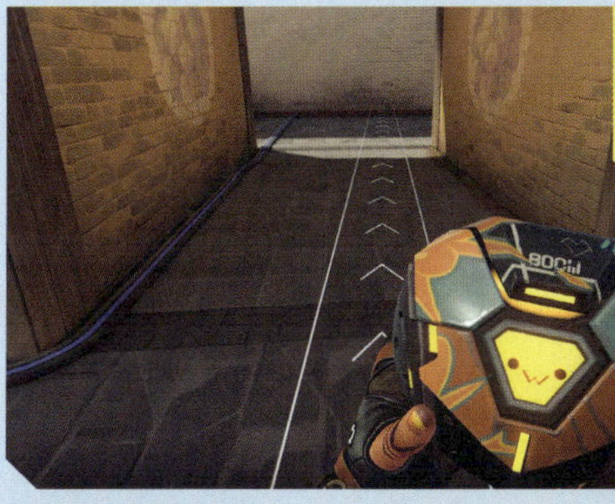

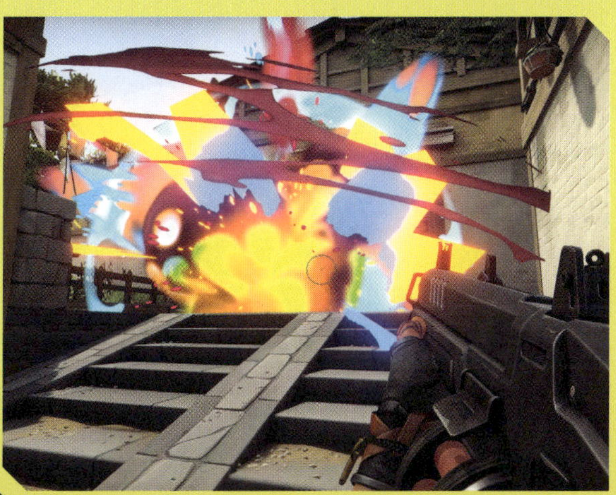

SHOWSTOPPER

For the final act, Raze steals the show by snatching a rocket launcher from her arsenal of gadgets and sending a rocket zooming off into the enemy lines. Whether she scores a direct hit or a glancing blow, the effect is the same – epic amounts of damage in a burst of beautiful colours.

REYNA

// DUELIST

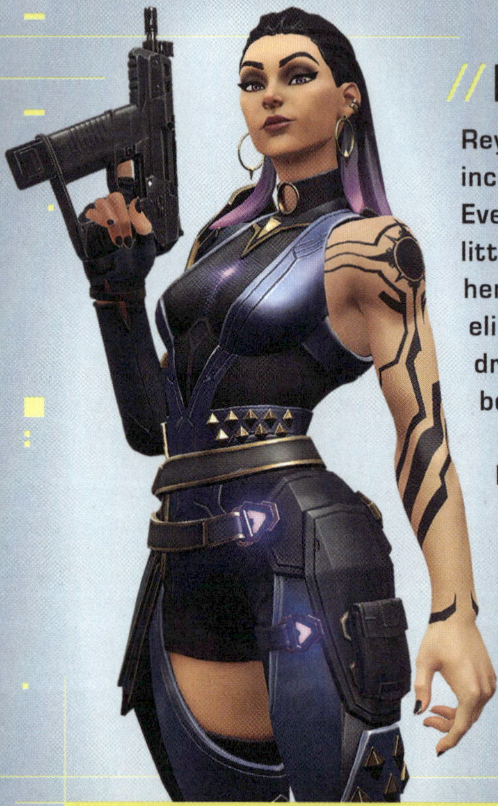

// BIOGRAPHY

Reyna uses her powers for trickery and increased performance when in battle. Everything is done with style, flair and a little bit of sass. Soul orbs are gifted to her from an unknown source after she eliminates an enemy, which Reyna can draw power from to turn invulnerable or boost her health.

Reyna is the deadly tip of an attacking rush, using blinds and deception to spring up where she isn't expected. She requires a decent amount of skill to master, but can prove to be a one-woman wave of terror to opposing teams. She's always dangerous and an asset to any squad.

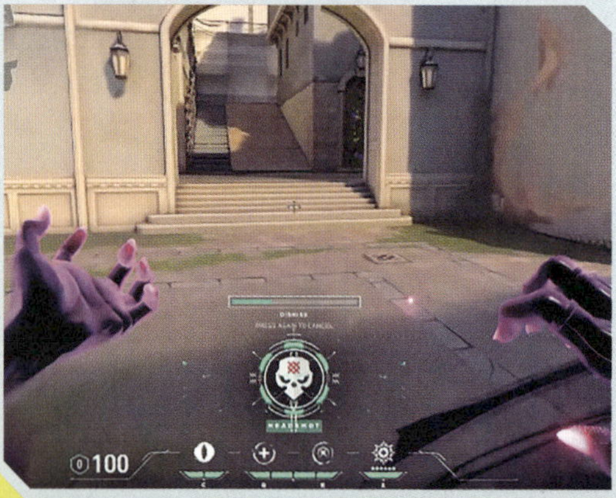

DISMISS

After consuming a soul orb, Reyna passes into another dimension for a few brief seconds, before reappearing on the battlefield. She can move as normal and spy on enemy movements while she traverses the unknown realm, and direct herself to cover so that she can reappear in a safe position.

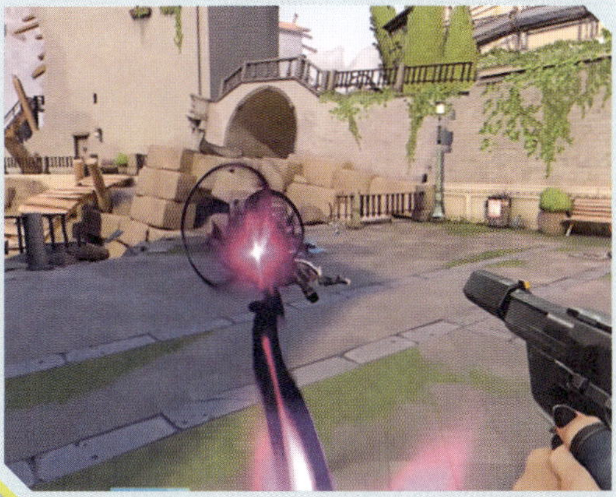

DEVOUR

Whenever Reyna kills an opponent, they leave behind a soul orb, which must be consumed within a few seconds. Any absorbed orb can be used to heal herself, rapidly restoring her health, even above the usual maximum, though this degrades quickly. If 'Empress' is active, orbs will automatically be consumed.

LEER

Casting an all-seeing eye to a fixed point, the leering eye blinds enemies who see it. The effect acts like a smoke screen unless the enemy looks away or destroys the eye. When combined with Dismiss, the enemy will never see Reyna coming for them.

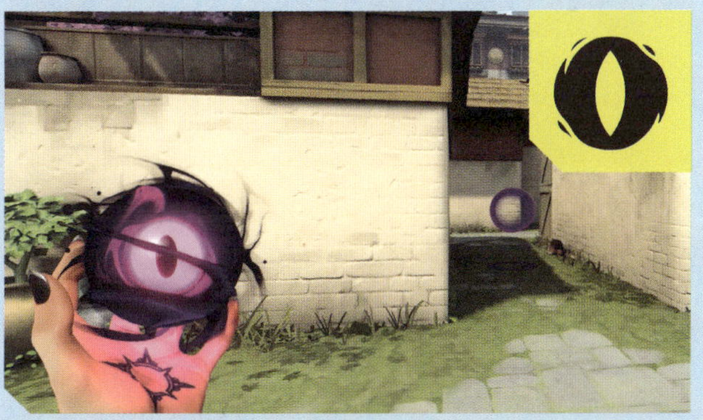

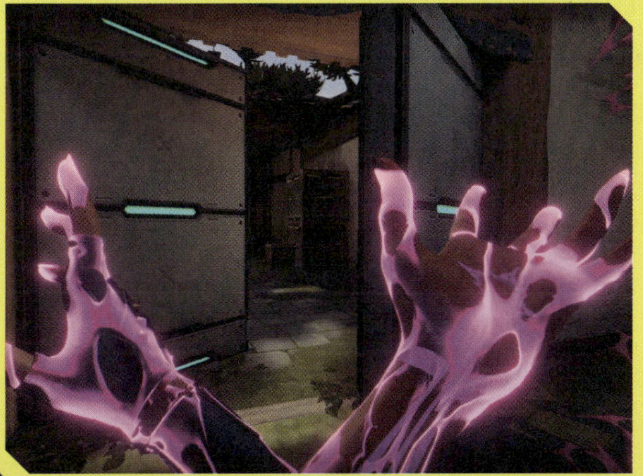

EMPRESS

Once Empress is activated, you better watch out! This ability sends Reyna into a frenzy, instantly increasing her rate of fire, weapon swap and reload speeds. With each successful kill, Reyna automatically slurps up the souls of her victims, which heals and extends the timer on the ability.

SAGE

// SENTINEL

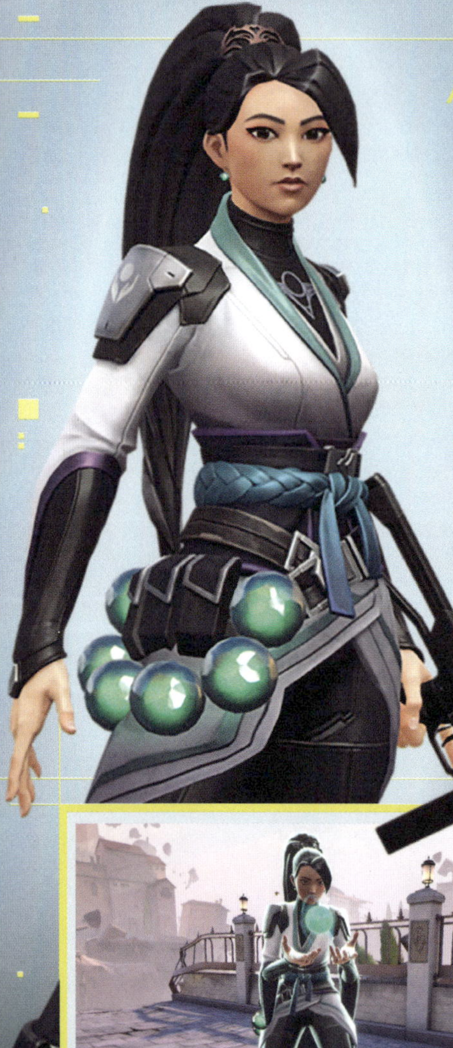

// BIOGRAPHY

Hailing from China in the Far East, Sage knows everything she needs to know about surviving on her own. Using her powers, she's able to protect teammates from the clutches of death or create helpful areas of effect that impede the enemy's progress into friendly territory.

When she's isn't holding back the enemy, Sage deploys orbs to heal members of her team, or bring them back from the brink of death if she's too late to protect them. Her orbs can also be used to create slowing splashes on the ground, or gigantic barriers that will soak up bullets and prevent enemies from gaining ground.

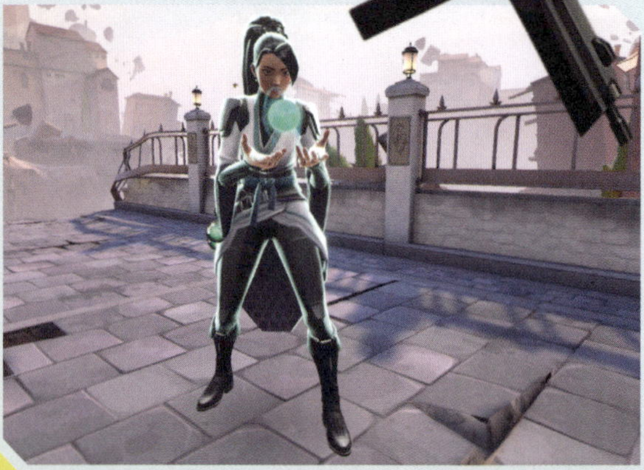

HEALING ORB

Firing this orb towards a teammate will cast a healing spell, restoring their health over time. Alternately, firing onto herself will cast the same spell, filling lost health points. Stick close by and Sage will see to it that her team lives to fight another day.

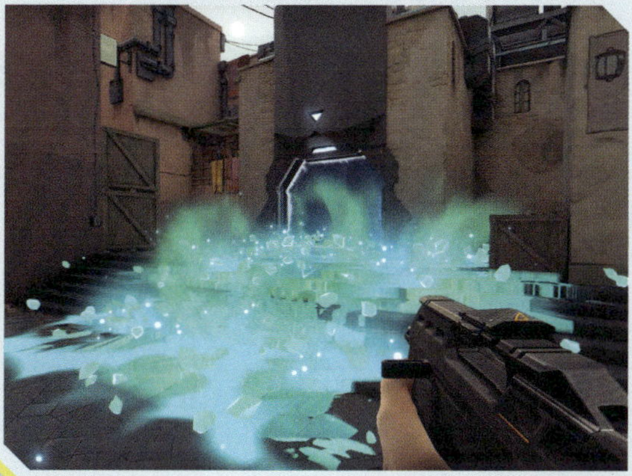

SLOW ORB

Need to hold off the enemy for a time while the team regathers their strength? Sage fires this ball of energy to the floor, creating an iced area that slows down anyone who walks over it. This can even be used on the spike site to halt the progress of a would-be defuser.

BARRIER ORB

Sometimes keeping the enemy at bay is the perfect solution and Sage is a master at building walls around her, blocking off entry points or shielding her team from bullets. If she summons the wall underneath her – or a teammate's – feet, it can raise the team to new heights – quite literally.

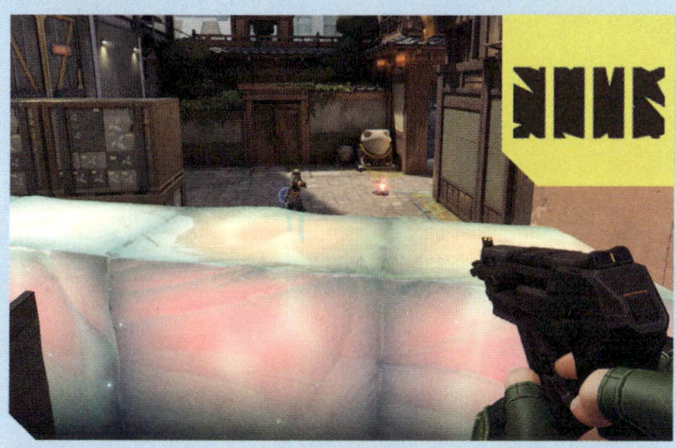

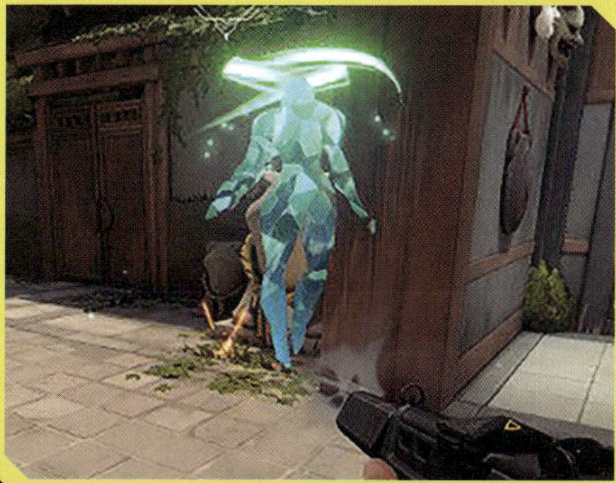

RESURRECTION

Pulling back a departing spirit takes time, but it's worth it to see her teammate back in the fight. Sage's ultimate cheats death, bringing one ally back to the battle and instantly tipping the scales back in her team's favour. It's wise to have someone covering you while you revive or you're both at risk.

SKYE

// INITIATOR

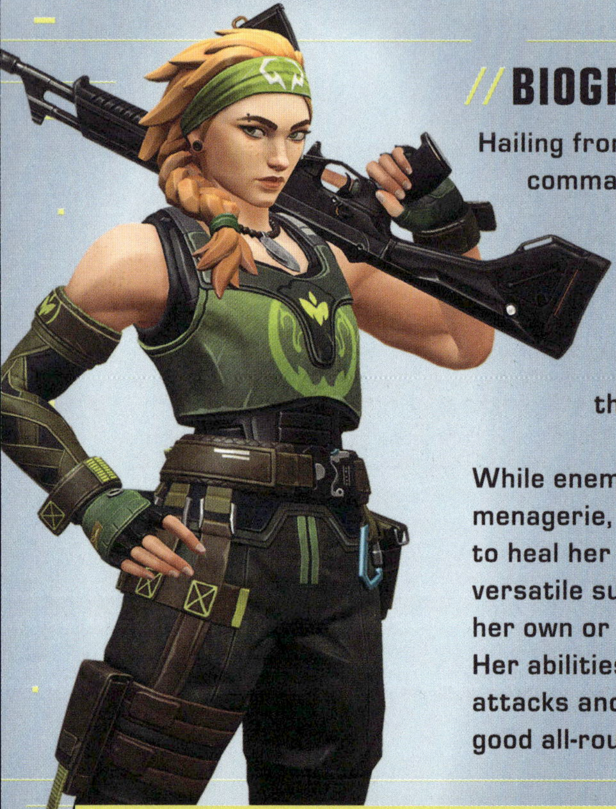

// BIOGRAPHY

Hailing from the Australian outback, Skye commands robotic versions of the animals that inhabit her native land. Her partnership with her metallic menagerie of animals means that she can have eyes and ears covering the battlefield in mere seconds.

While enemies are distracted by Skye's menagerie, she uses the time wisely; to heal her team and cover angles. A versatile support, Skye can work on her own or as a solid part of the team. Her abilities are a nice mixture of heals, attacks and debuffs, which makes her a good all-rounder.

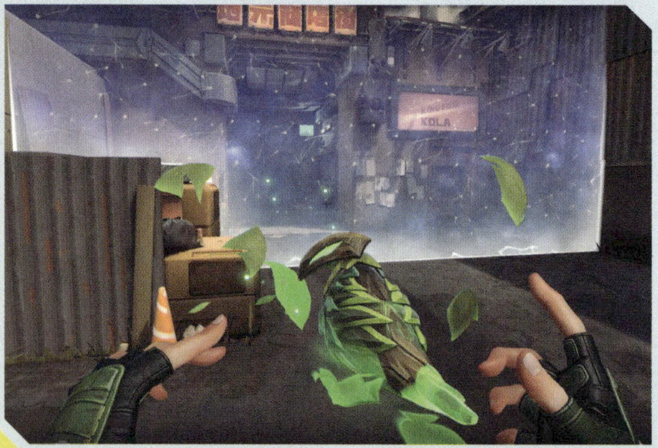

GUIDING LIGHT

Creating a hawk trinket, Skye guides the bird into battle. Guided by moving the crosshair, the hawk swoops into view of enemies before bursting into a ball of light, blinding them to incoming action. Perfect for holding back an enemy advance.

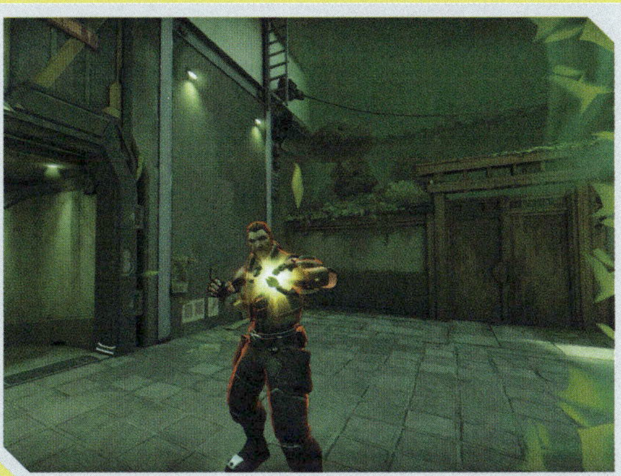

TRAILBLAZER

Holding a trinket of a Tasmanian tiger, Skye conjures the beast to fight. When the tiger appears, Skye takes control of its vision and body, guiding the feline towards enemies. As the tiger leaps forward, it explodes into a concussive blast, pushing the enemy backwards while dealing them damage.

REGROWTH

Skye's memories of the Australian plant life are the basis of her healing ability. Skye channels the energy found within living plants and diverts it to her team. Though Skye cannot heal herself, she can use her healing pool to fix up the wounds of any team member in range and line of sight.

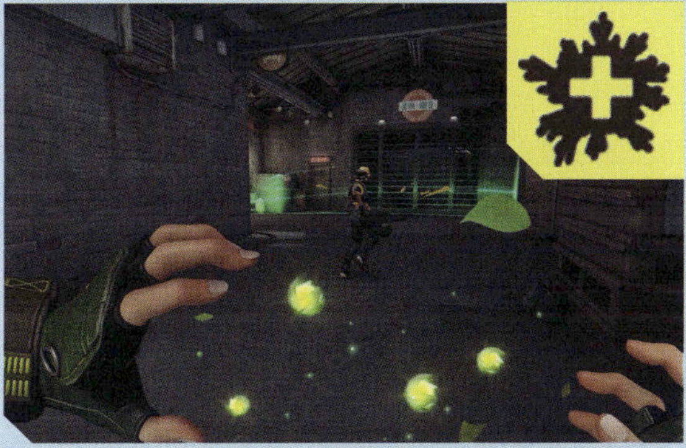

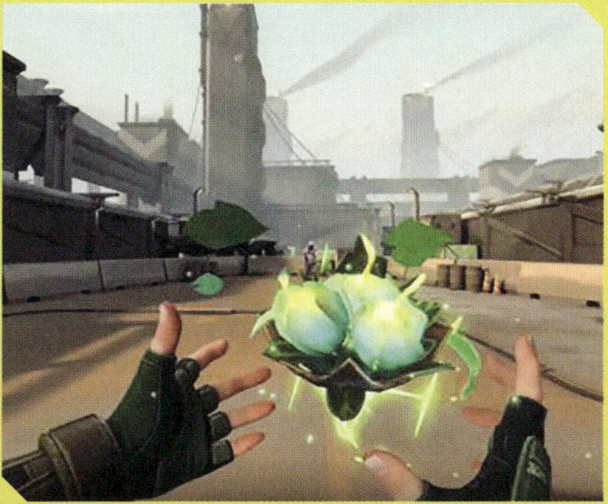

SEEKERS

Not much is known about the Seekers. Is it a plant? Or something from Skye's mind? When conjured, Skye launches three Seekers out into the field to track down enemies and attach to them. Once attached, the Seeker applies 'nearsight' to an enemy, which reduces their vision range. Very helpful when combined with a sniper rifle.

SOVA

// INITIATOR

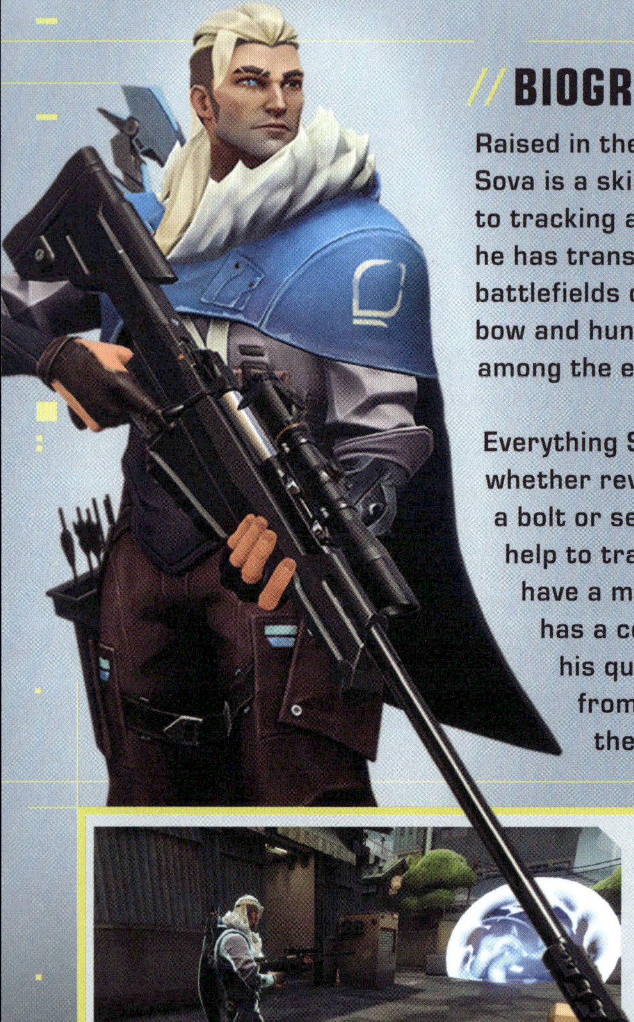

// BIOGRAPHY

Raised in the wintry tundras of Russia, Sova is a skilled hunter. More accustomed to tracking animals in his motherland, he has transferred his skills to the battlefields of Valorant, where he uses his bow and hunting skills to find new prey among the enemy squad.

Everything Sova does is from range – whether revealing enemy positions with a bolt or sending out a drone. His skills help to track enemies, so they never have a moment's peace. However, he has a couple of offensive arrows in his quiver that make him a threat from afar. If Sova is on the field, they can run, but they can't hide.

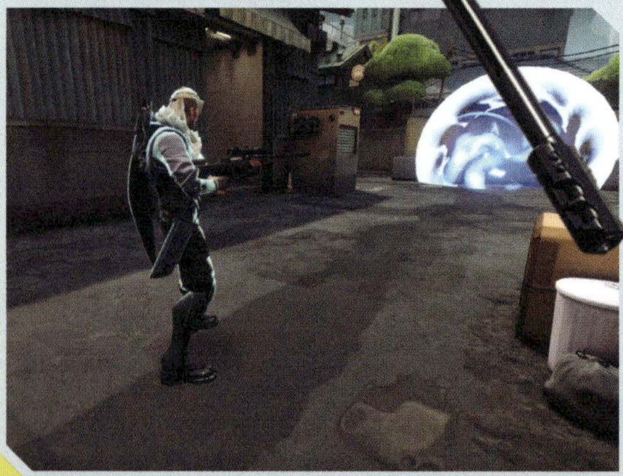

RECON BOLT

Holding the ability key, Sova pulls back on his bow to fire an arrow that embeds itself in a surface, monitoring passers-by. When an enemy moves within the arrow's range, it signals Sova and his teammates. Using the Alternate Fire button, you can also add up to two bounces to a shot.

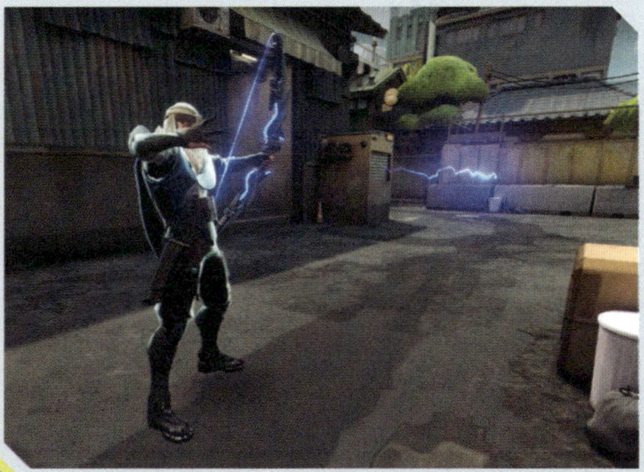

SHOCK BOLT

Pulling this arrow from its quiver and firing it at a target will produce a sphere of electricity. Bursting into a ball of frazzling bolts, this ability will quickly damage opponents and can be bounced off walls too, allowing it to reach awkward – or well-guarded – spots.

OWL DRONE

Sova takes control of an owl drone and flies it around the battlefield, surveying enemy positions from a safe distance. While this allows him to tell his team where enemies may be holed up, he can also fire a tracking dart into an unsuspecting foe, revealing their location to all.

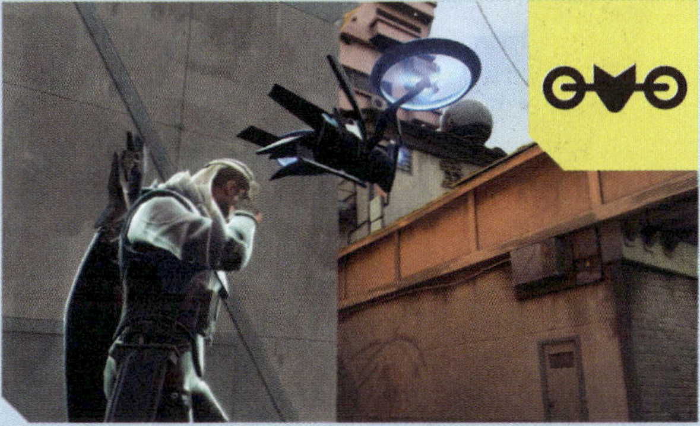

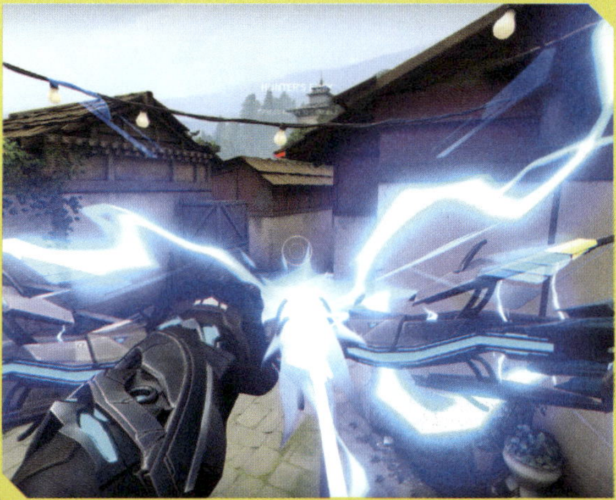

HUNTER'S FURY

Once active, Sova has a short amount of time to fire a trio of electric arrows, which can pass through walls to hit opponents. Not only does this volley do damage on contact, but it marks the locations of any enemies in its path. There's a short window of time to use all three arrows, but it should be more than enough.

VIPER

// CONTROLLER

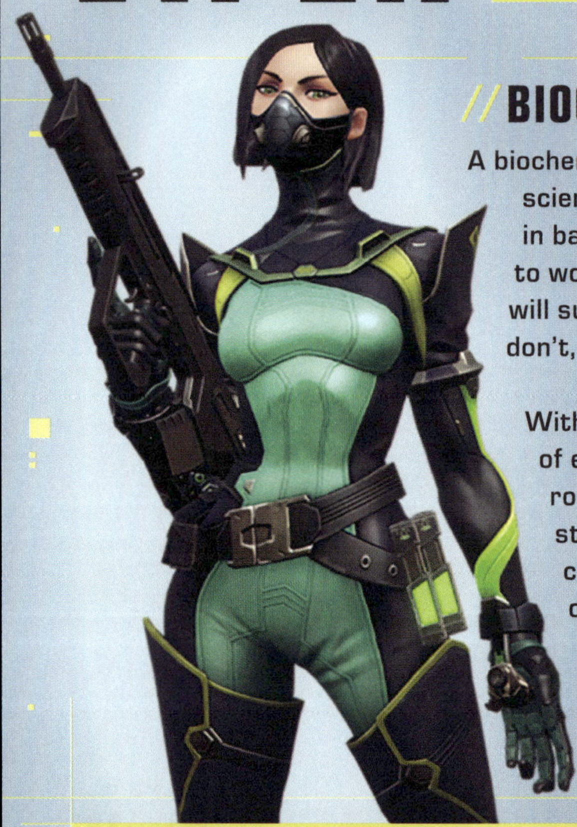

// BIOGRAPHY

A biochemist by trade, Viper uses her scientific know-how to neutralise foes in battle. As her poisonous toxins go to work on the enemy faction, they will surely lose their minds. And if they don't, Viper will take them by force.

With poison clouds and lots of area of effect abilities, Viper is a good all-round agent who excels in causing steady damage on a mass scale. She can deploy her toxins in a variety of forms: domes, long screens and liquids. If an enemy speeds around the corner into her noxious gas, they'll be feeling the effects for a while after.

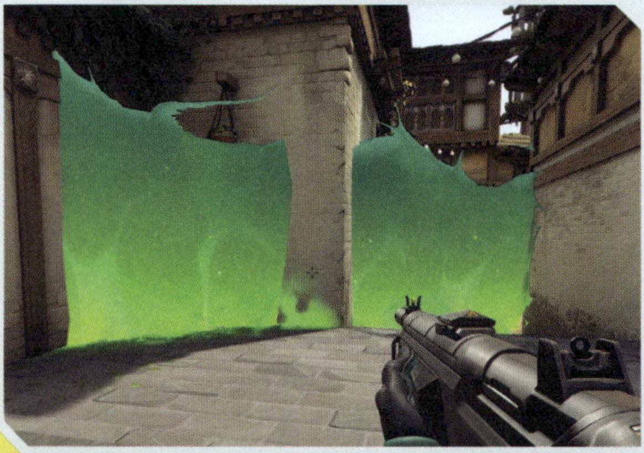

TOXIC SCREEN

Viper has to keep an eye on her fuel gauge when using toxic screen. After firing a long line of gas dispensers, the fuel will run down as a wall of poison fills the air, blocking lines of sight and also damaging anyone foolish enough to try and walk through.

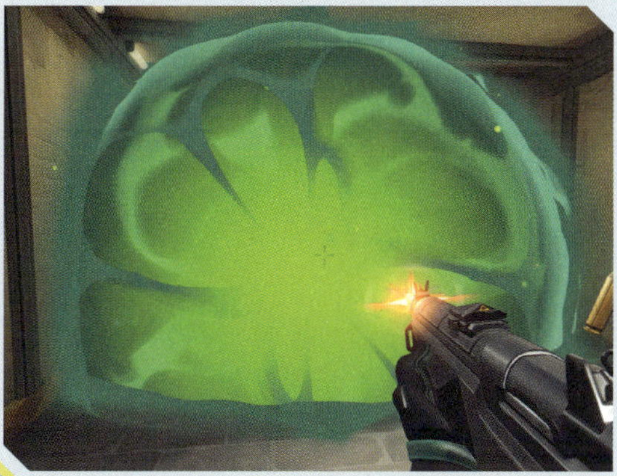

POISON CLOUD

With this ability, Viper places a contraption that can, on her command, disperse a ball of her signature toxin. It will consume fuel if left active, but can be toggled on and off by activating the ability. Any enemy in this zone will suffer damage over time, until they're clear of the smog.

SNAKE BITE

Viper has her own explosive canisters to play around with, but rather than paint or fire, hers are filled with liquid poison that slows and damages enemies. It can be used to cover choke points to hold back a rushing team, or to damage them as they pass through, handing you a weaker target.

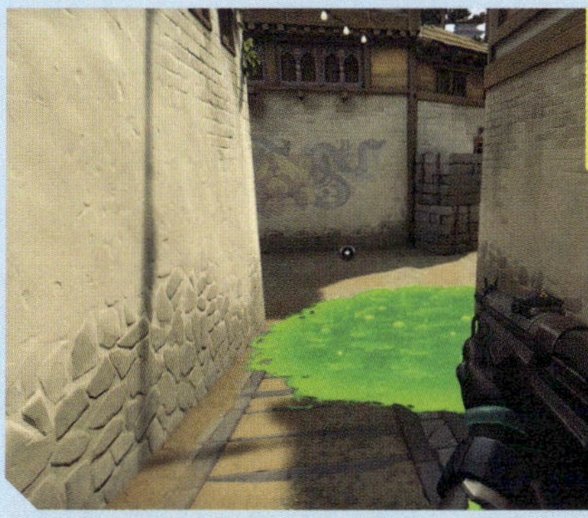

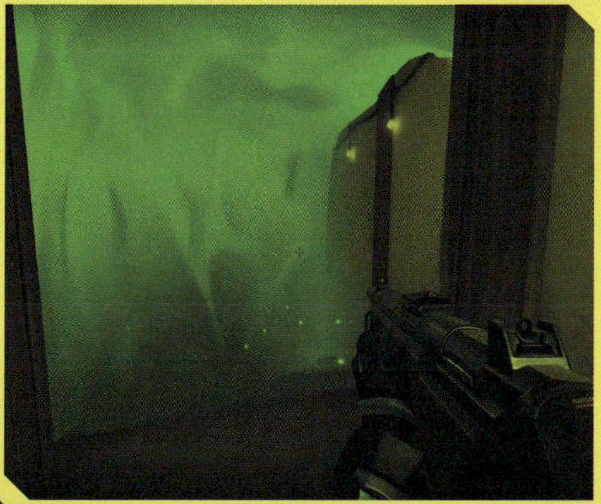

VIPER'S PIT

For her ultimate, Viper oozes gas from her hands, spreading a miasma of poison around a large area. Within this dome of toxins, enemies suffer a reduced range of sight due to the thick clouds. It also erodes the opponent's maximum health, slowly reducing it to 1hp, making them easier to eliminate as Viper strikes at the enemy.

GAMEPLAY

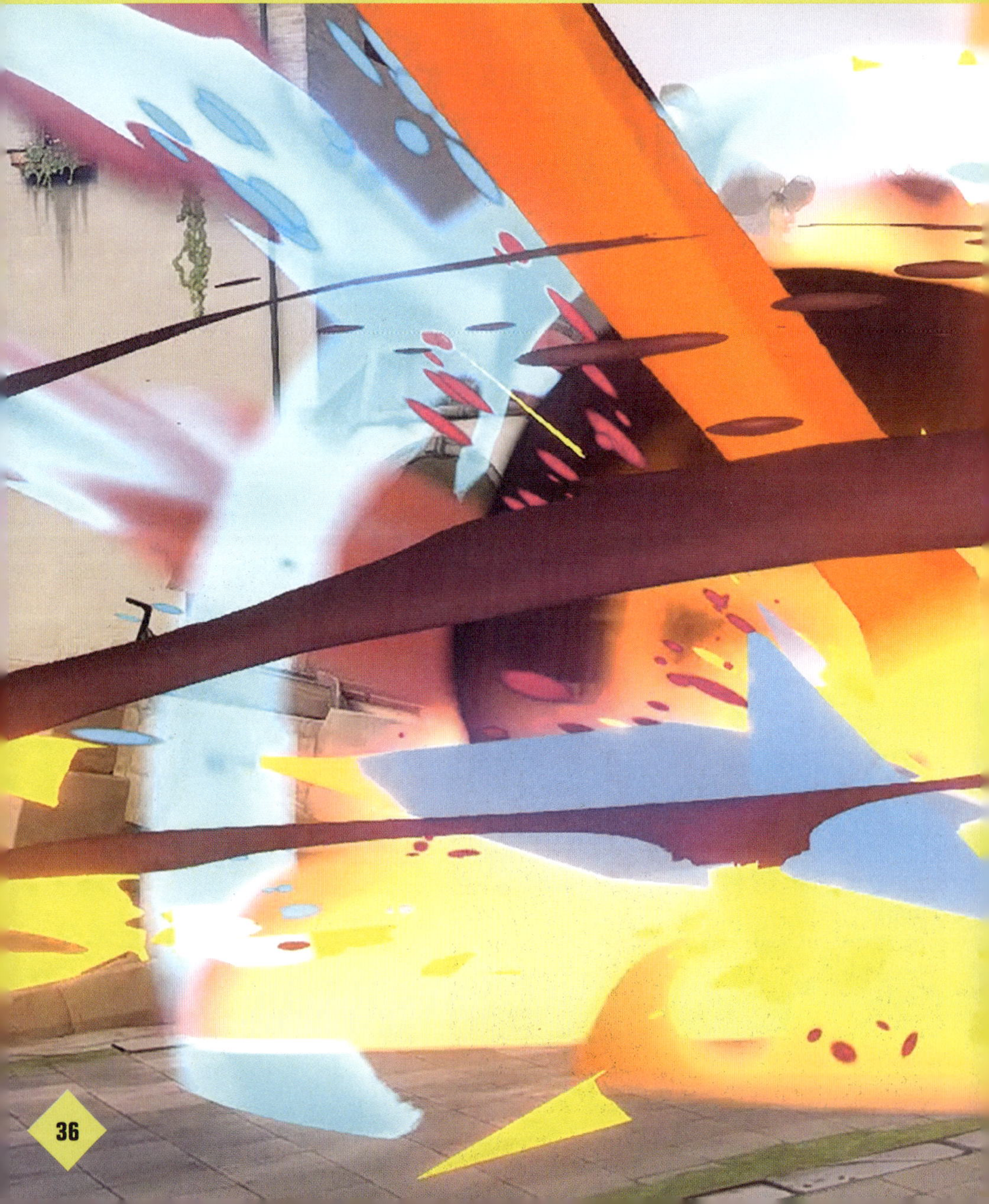

Now you've met the agents, it's time to fight. The arsenal of weapons at your disposal is huge and affects how you approach a round and supplement your character's skills. Using money you earn from kills and round wins is also an important tactic to consider. In this section, we'll take a deeper look at every weapon, and discover some key tactics about how to move around the maps and use your abilities.

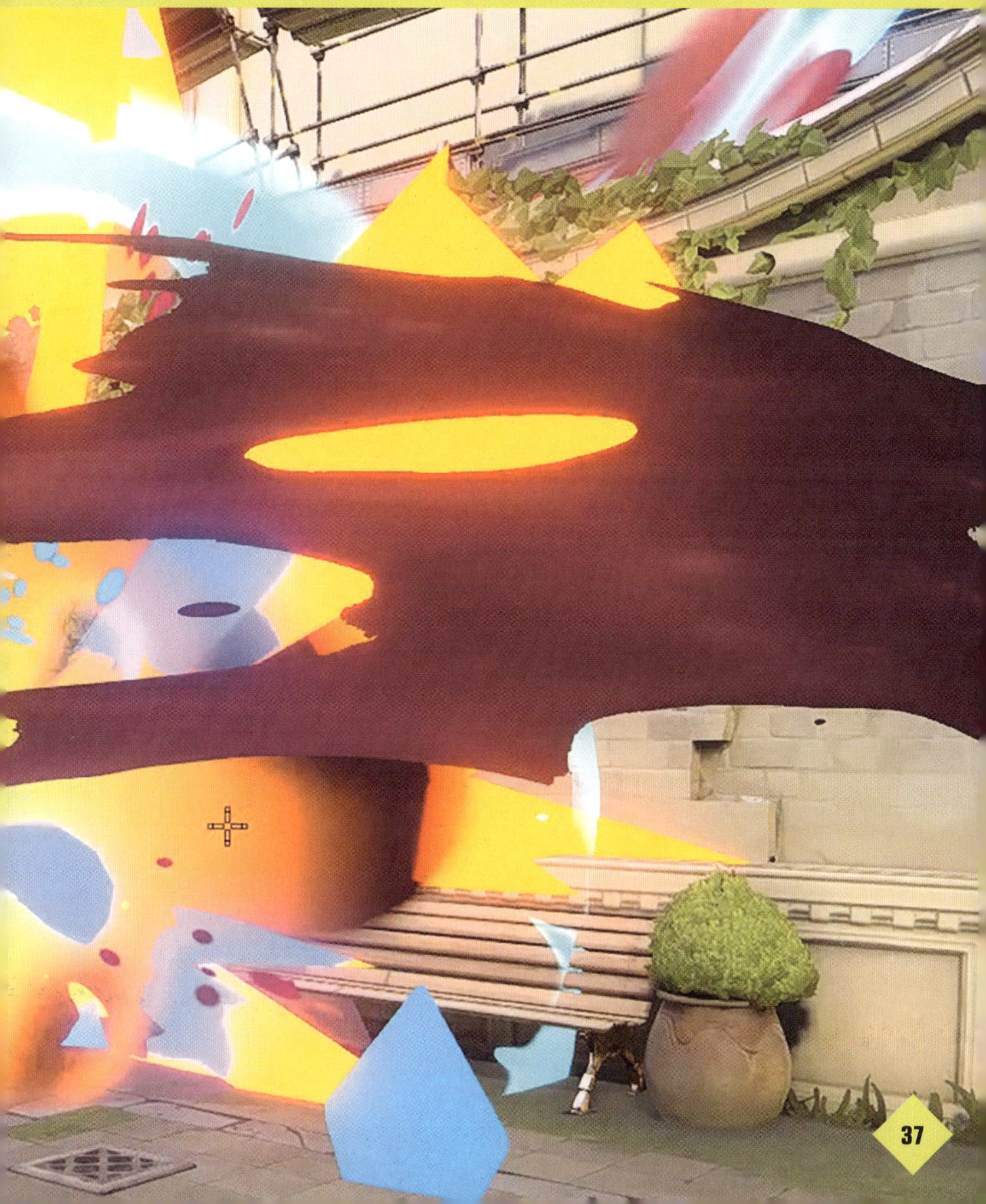

THE BUY PHASE

There are FOUR ways to earn credits:

- Killing an enemy
- Planting the spike
- Winning a round
- Losing streak

Your agent card is in the top left corner of the buy screen and shows how many credits you currently have, along with a few communication prompts for buying strategies.

Down the left side of your screen, you'll see the agent cards of all your teammates, showing how many creds they have, and the weapons they're equipping.

You can 'right-click' any gun to ask your teammates to buy it for you if you're struggling for creds. Remember to be kind and help where you can, it might just win you the round.

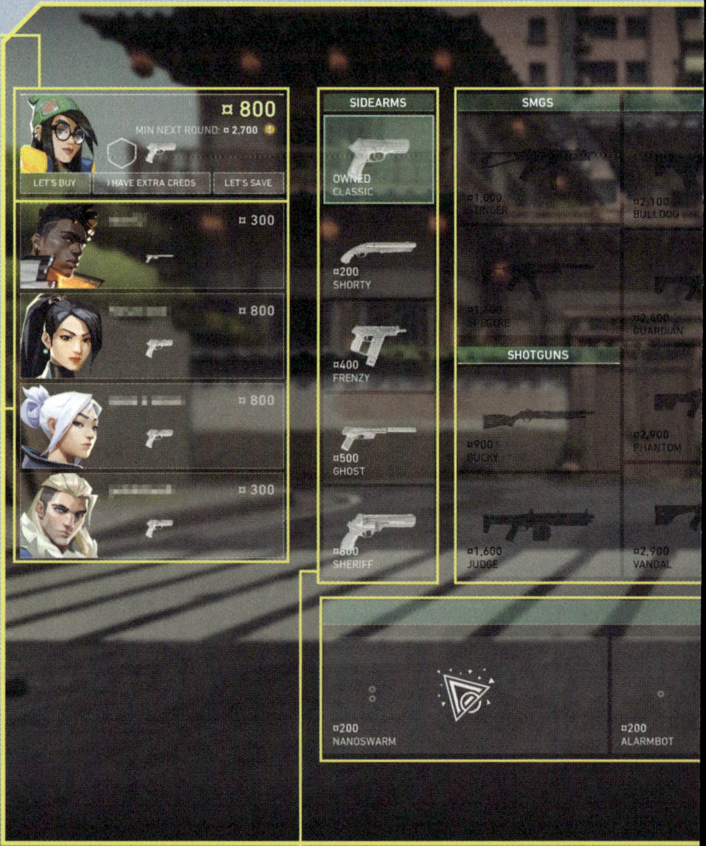

This column has the sidearms, which are secondary weapons you can equip. Everyone starts with the Classic for free, but can replace it with any other sidearm for a cost.

The first stage of any round is the Buy Phase. Before the action begins, you're given an opportunity to use credits to purchase the gear you want to use in the next round – press 'B' to bring up the buy screen. You earn credits after every round and will enter the Buy Phase before each round begins.

The main part of the screen is taken up by the primary weapons, split into their relevant categories. You'll see a credit cost for each weapon, and can left-click to buy the weapon if you have enough credits available.

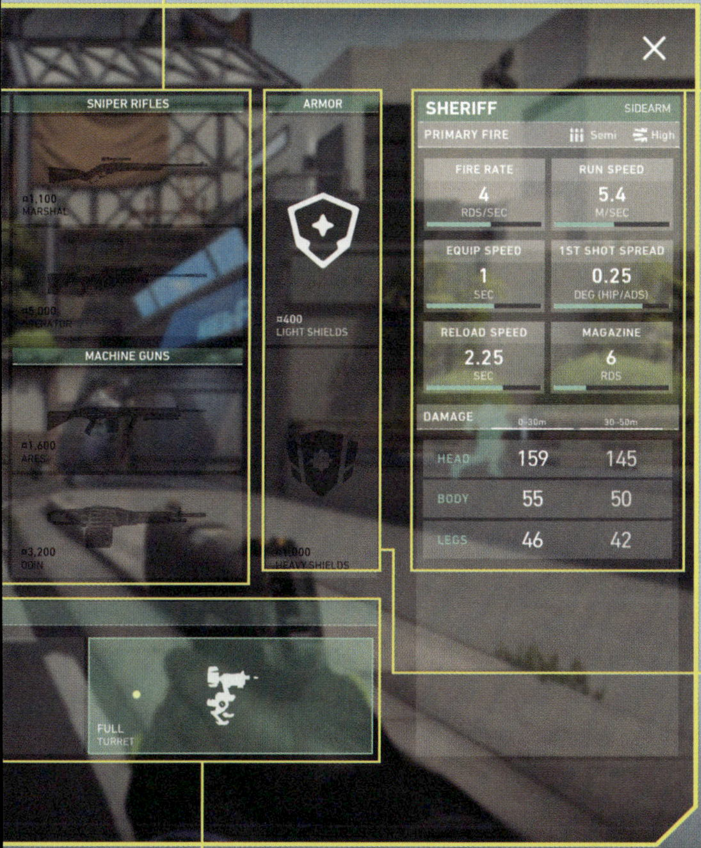

When you select a weapon, a sidebar will appear showing its stats. This is useful for quickly comparing guns and how well they suit your style of play.

There are two shield options – light and heavy. The light option is more economical, but if you have the creds to spare you may as well upgrade to the heavy for additional protection.

At the bottom of the screen, you'll see your agent's abilities and the cost to buy them. Some agents get abilities free each round, like Omen, while others have to top theirs up by buying most of them, like Brimstone.

THE ARSENAL

// SIDEARMS

A good sidearm can take you a long way in Valorant, especially if your aim is good. It's best to look at them as back-up guns most of the time, when you're reloading or have run out of ammo for your primary weapon. They're great for 'eco' rounds where you want to save credits for later.

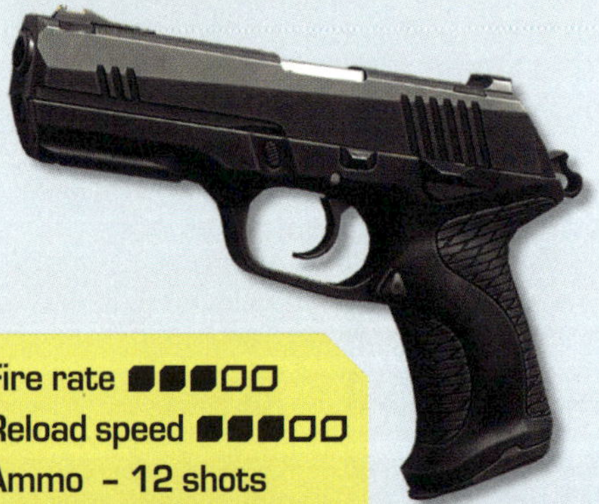

CLASSIC

The standard handgun you get for free in every round is accurate but lacks power. Even landing a headshot won't outright eliminate your opponent. For a pistol round, you might want to choose something with a bit more bite in each shot, otherwise you may be outmatched. It has a secondary fire that shoots three bullets in an erratic spray which is more useful at close-quarters.

Fire rate ■■■□□
Reload speed ■■■□□
Ammo - 12 shots
Damage ■■□□□

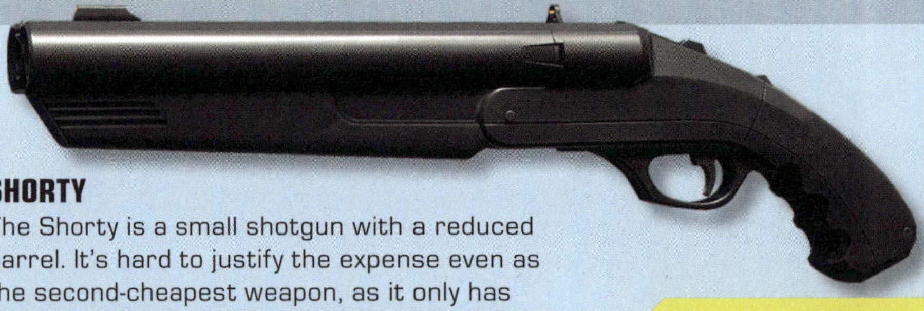

SHORTY

The Shorty is a small shotgun with a reduced barrel. It's hard to justify the expense even as the second-cheapest weapon, as it only has two rounds, yet causes huge damage with headshots. It can take enemies by surprise, but you might be left high and dry reloading a second later.

Fire rate ■■□□□
Reload speed ■■■□□
Ammo - 2 shots
Damage ■□□□□

FRENZY

This compact SMG delivers rapid bursts, which makes it more potent than most sidearms, but tougher to aim. With a high rate of fire and decent damage with each hit, the Frenzy is great at short range. You'll want to fire it in bursts in order to stay accurate. Holding the trigger down will send shots everywhere and quickly leave you needing a reload.

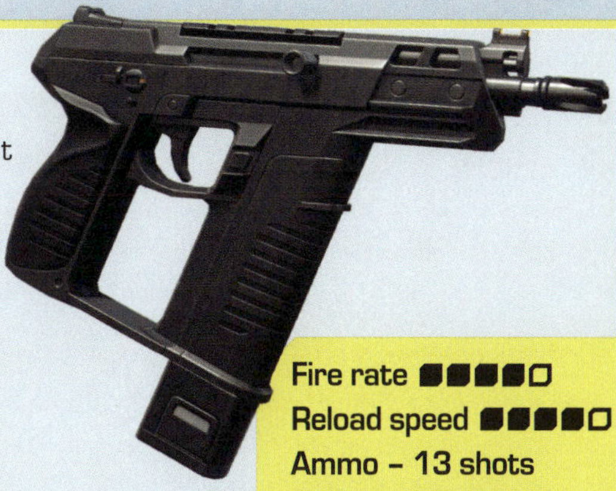

Fire rate ■■■■□
Reload speed ■■■■□
Ammo – 13 shots
Damage ■□□□□

GHOST

The only silent sidearm is the Ghost. Many pros choose this weapon as it hits hard – a headshot is an instant kill if the enemy has no armour – and it can't be heard as well as other weapons. The Ghost also has no tracer fire, which means there is no visual cue of where the bullet came from.

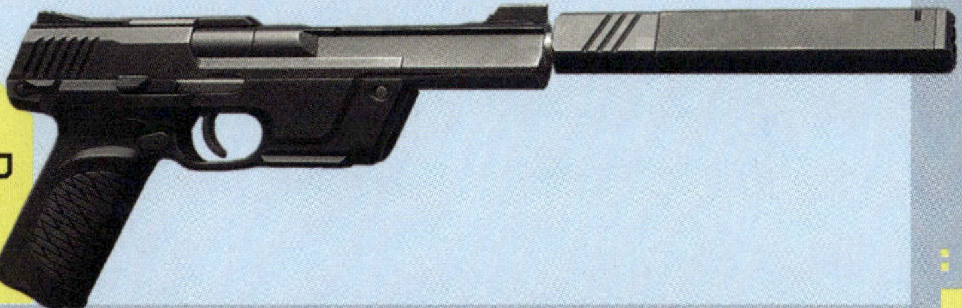

Fire rate ■■■□□
Reload speed ■■■■□
Ammo – 15 shots
Damage ■■■■□

SHERIFF

There is no sidearm more powerful than the Sheriff – it packs a heck of a punch, even at a distance. The damage halves when hitting the body or legs, so if you're inaccurate, it might be a waste of creds. Two headshots will take out a fully armoured enemy with ease, but the penalty is the low rate of fire and the long reload speed. If you can deal with that, the Sheriff is an easy pick.

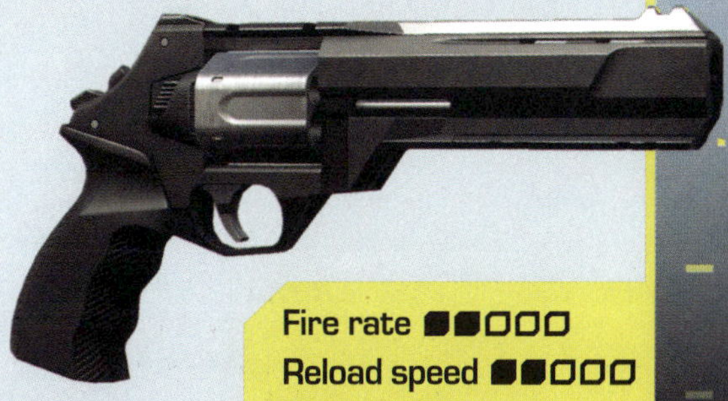

Fire rate ■■□□□
Reload speed ■■□□□
Ammo – 6 shots
Damage ■■■■■

THE ARSENAL

// SMGS/SHOTGUNS

Choosing between an SMG or shotgun is very situational and dependent on how you like to play. Players who like to move fast often have better luck with an SMG, compared to those who like to camp or sneak up for a close-range shotgun blast.

STINGER

The Stinger is a burst-fire SMG, which fires four shots on each pull of the trigger. As with any SMG, it's a fast weapon, but lacks damage; it will take several body shots to finish an enemy and it's only slightly better when aiming for the head. Aiming down its sights with the right mouse button will stabilise your aim and tighten the spread of bullets fired.

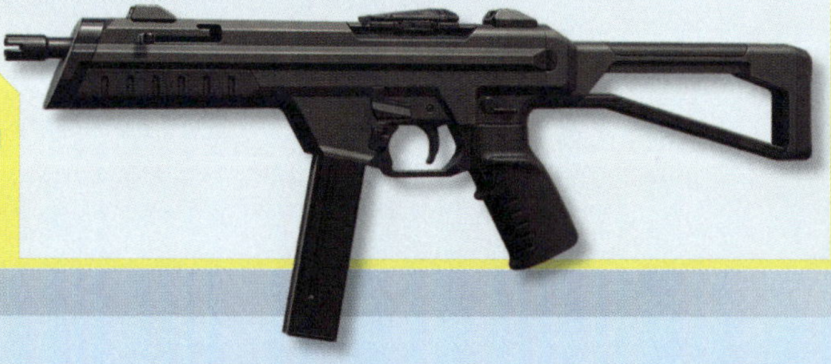

Fire rate ■■■■■
Reload speed ■■■□□
Ammo – 20 shots
Damage ■■□□□

SPECTRE

The slower rate of fire from the Spectre is the cost of a higher damage output than the Stinger, plus it's silenced, which makes it a stealthier option. As with the Ghost, there is no tracer fire and shots are unheard at range, making this brilliant for outflanking your enemy and taking them by surprise. A bigger ammo clip also means you can take more shots before finding cover to reload.

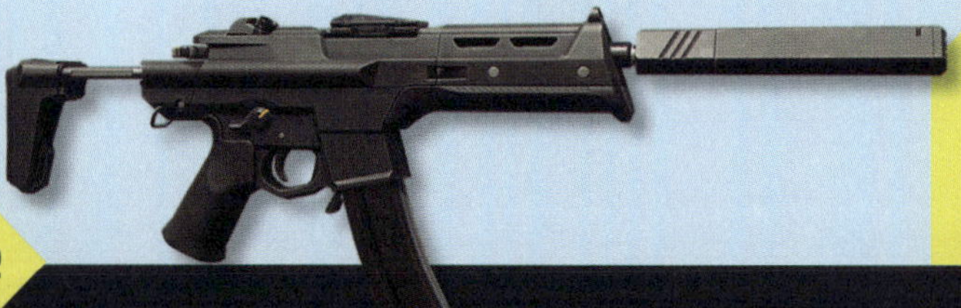

Fire rate ■■■■□
Reload speed ■■■■■
Ammo – 30 shots
Damage ■■□□□

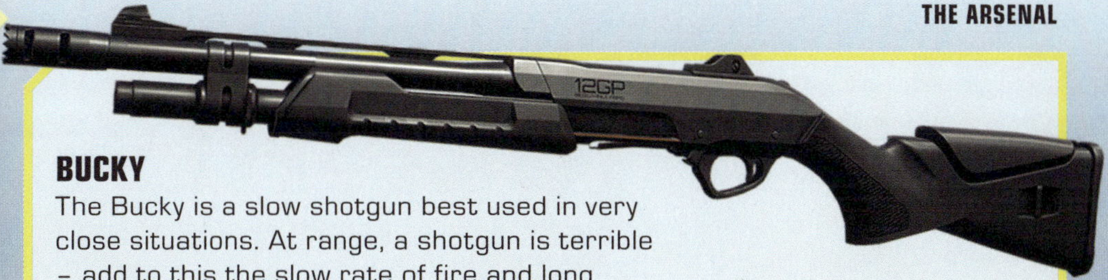

BUCKY

The Bucky is a slow shotgun best used in very close situations. At range, a shotgun is terrible – add to this the slow rate of fire and long reload times. However, it's great for a wide spray of bullets that can hit multiple enemies. The Bucky also has a neat trick up its sleeve too. The Alternate Fire mode blasts a canister that explodes in a hail of deadly shots, causing a wider range of damage.

Fire rate ■□□□□
Reload speed ■■□□□
Ammo – 5 shots
Damage ■■□□□

JUDGE

If you want a faster rate of fire from a shotgun, call on the Judge. It's an automatic, so if you hold down the trigger it will keep firing until the barrel is empty. It holds more shots than the Bucky but does less damage. Get up-close, hold your position and fire until the enemy hits the ground.

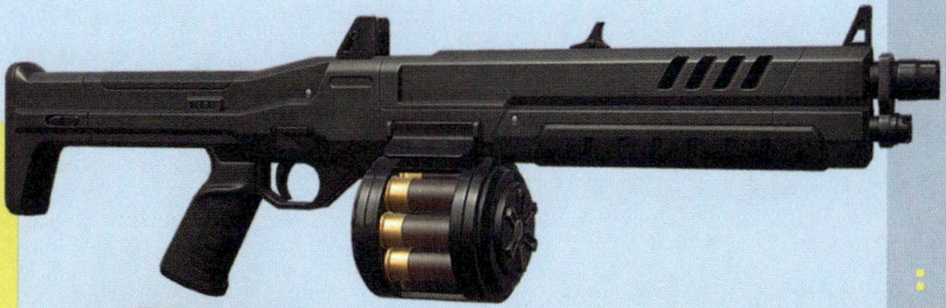

Fire rate ■■■□□
Reload speed ■■□□□
Ammo – 7 shots
Damage ■□□□□

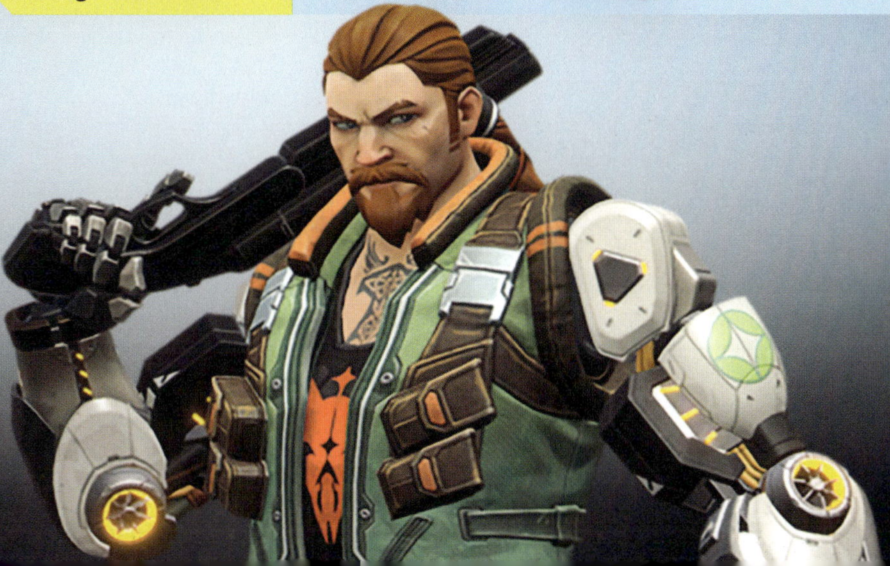

THE ARSENAL

// RIFLES

Rifles are great all-rounders. They're reliable at range and the damage output is good enough that you'll be able to snipe enemies from any distance. They do have their flaws – wild recoil, slower rates of fire and long reload times – but they're often brandished by most players on the battlefield.

BULLDOG

As the cheapest rifle in the selection, the Bulldog is a good starting point. A 3-round burst means the damage can be slightly higher than other rifles, but for base damage per shot, this is the weakest. A good rate of fire and reload speed will mean you can pick your shots, but the non-automatic fire mode can be a barrier to some players.

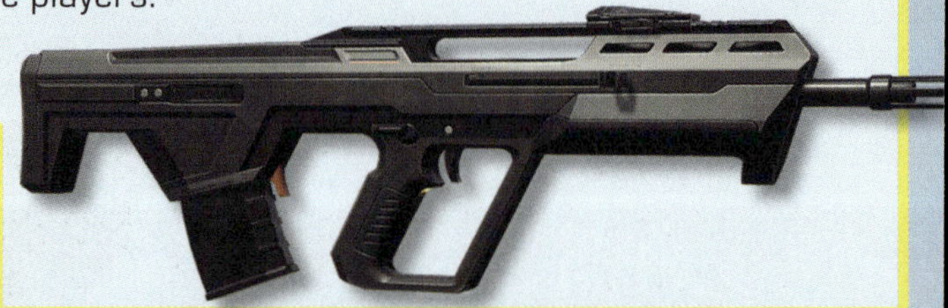

Fire rate ■■■□□
Reload speed ■■■□□
Ammo – 24 shots
Damage ■■■□□

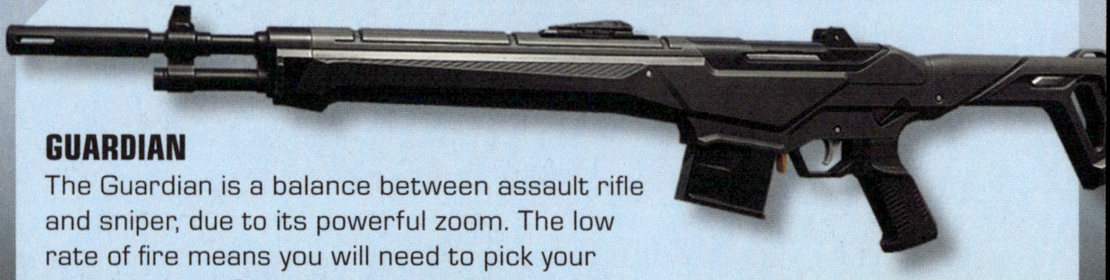

GUARDIAN

The Guardian is a balance between assault rifle and sniper, due to its powerful zoom. The low rate of fire means you will need to pick your shots, but the Guardian is all about accuracy. The zoom can cause some problems with vision if aimed at nearby targets, and it is difficult to shoot from the hip, but it does have the highest damage of any rifle.

Fire rate ■■□□□
Reload speed ■■■□□
Ammo – 12 shots
Damage ■■■■■

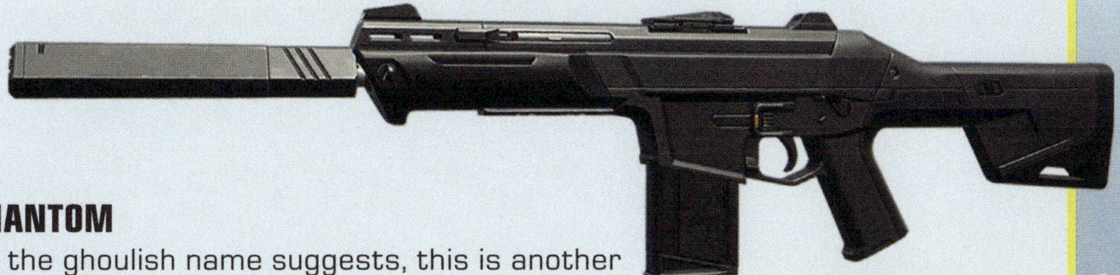

PHANTOM

As the ghoulish name suggests, this is another silenced weapon, which means no tracers and less sound from shots – a bonus for sneakier players. However, it does have a drop off in damage if you're far away from a target. You'll want to get close and pepper your enemy with plenty of shots.

Fire rate ■■■■□
Reload speed ■■■□□
Ammo – 30 shots
Damage ■■■□□

VANDAL

The Vandal is a fan favourite. It's got decent damage, with no drop-off for distance, and the rate of fire means you can keep the pressure on enemies. As with any rifle, recoil is a problem if not used in bursts, but it generally has a tighter spray than other rifles. The fully automatic nature of the gun makes it as great for hipfiring as it is for shooting from a distance.

Fire rate ■■■□□
Reload speed ■■■□□
Ammo – 25 shots
Damage ■■■■□

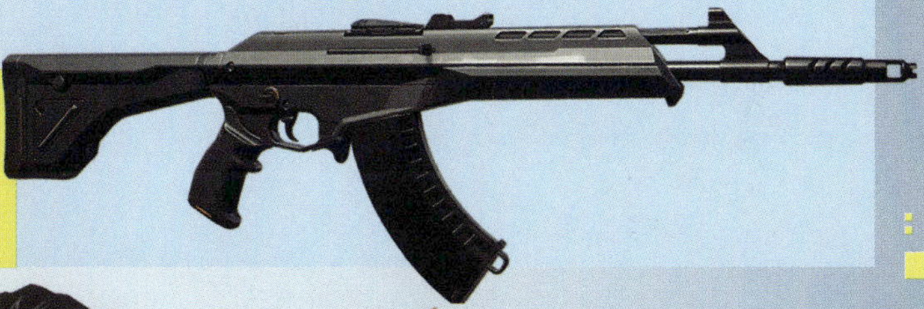

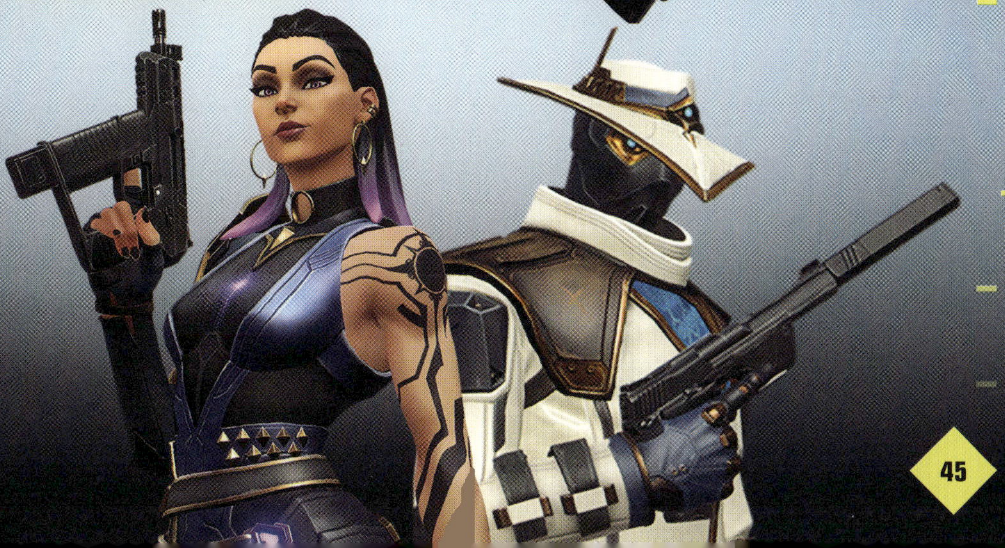

THE ARSENAL

// SNIPERS, MACHINE GUNS AND ARMOUR

Rounding out our overview of the weapons are sniper rifles and machine guns – two arms that deliver massive damage, but in very different ways. The sniper is a devastating weapon from range and requires a steady hand, while machine guns unleash an erratic torrent of bullets at targets. Armour gives you extra defence too.

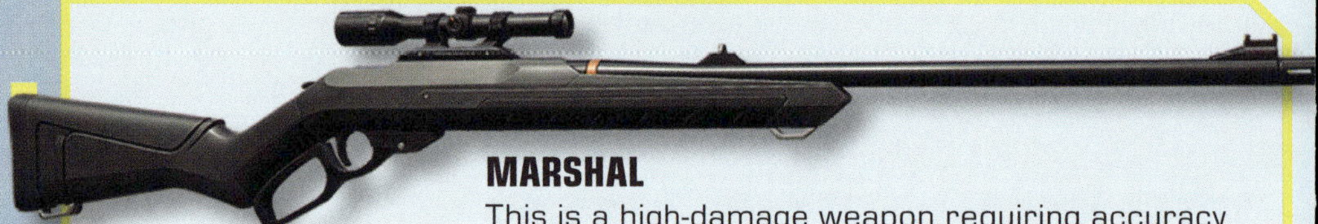

MARSHAL

This is a high-damage weapon requiring accuracy and patience. It can easily kill an enemy in one shot to the head, even if they have full armour. But if you miss your shot, it will take time to compensate for recoil and take the next one. They're relatively redundant if you're caught up-close against an SMG or rifle, so they're best when you're positioned at the back of a site you're defending.

Fire rate ■□□□□
Reload speed ■■■□□
Ammo – 5 shots
Damage ■■■■■

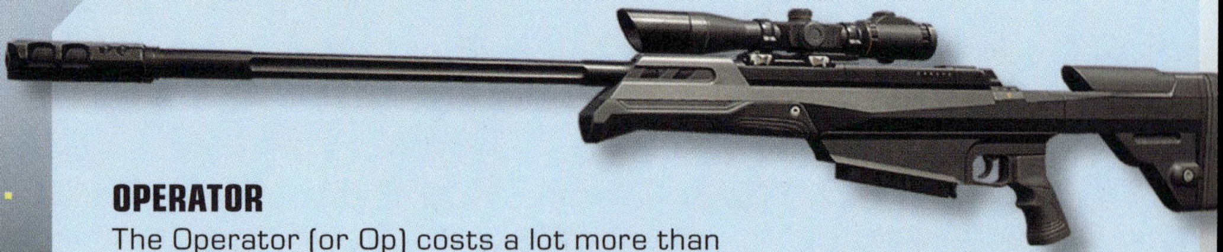

OPERATOR

The Operator (or Op) costs a lot more than the Marshal due to the changeable zoom and high 'damage through cover' stats. Another bonus to this gun is its rate of fire, which allows you to land consecutive shots from a single scoping. They're perfect for holding down narrow walkways if you can land headshots.

Fire rate ■□□□□
Reload speed ■■□□□
Ammo – 5 shots
Damage ■■■■■

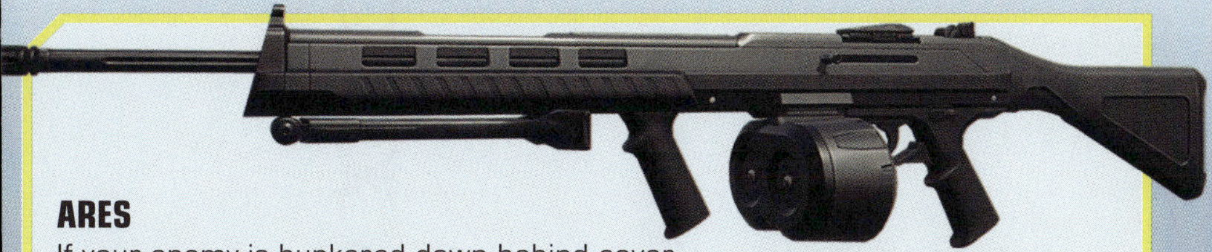

ARES

If your enemy is hunkered down behind cover, you can let loose with the Ares and penetrate walls to drive them out, or cause fast, consistent damage to enemies in the open. The Ares is the cheaper of the machine guns, but reloads faster. Machine guns are heavy, so your speed will drop with this gun.

Fire rate ■■■■■
Reload speed ■■■□□
Ammo – 50 shots
Damage ■■■□□

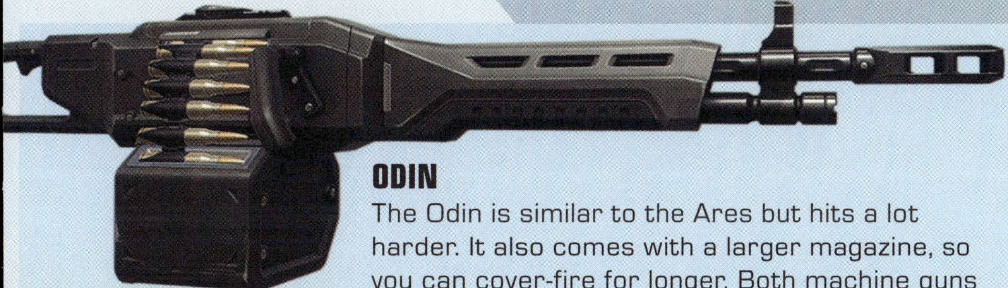

ODIN

The Odin is similar to the Ares but hits a lot harder. It also comes with a larger magazine, so you can cover-fire for longer. Both machine guns have reduced damage at longer distances, but if you're holding an angle, it doesn't matter. The Odin's damage output ramps up as you continue to shoot, so if you can handle the recoil, it becomes increasingly more deadly over time.

Fire rate ■■■■■
Reload speed ■□□□□
Ammo – 100 shots
Damage ■■■□□

ARMOUR

Armour comes in two sizes and is automatically worn when bought. Shields absorb 66% of the damage your agent receives, with the light shield breaking after it has taken 25 points of damage and the heavy version breaking after 50 points of damage. The light version is more economical, but if you can afford it, the added protection of heavy armour is worth the investment.

LIGHT SHIELD

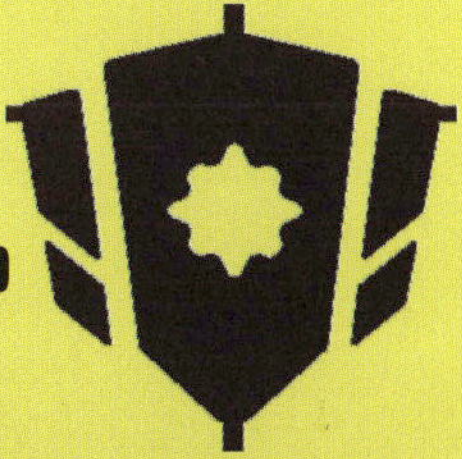

HEAVY SHIELD

ABILITY TACTICS

The balance between gunplay and tactics is finely tuned – if you rely on one without the other, you're likely to wind up on the losing team. Knowing when and where to use your agent's abilities is a huge part of the game, but you also need to know what other agents are capable of, so you can coordinate with your team and counter enemies.

KNOW YOUR ROLE

You can break down agents by the roles that they fill, defined by the abilities they use. For example, Sage is primarily a healer, so she's more of a support agent, while Raze and Phoenix have damage-dealing skills that make them potent offensive characters. Figuring out where your agent excels will allow you to make better use of their abilities.

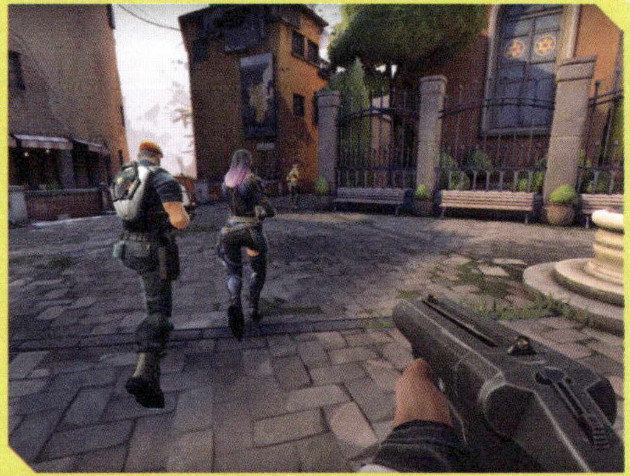

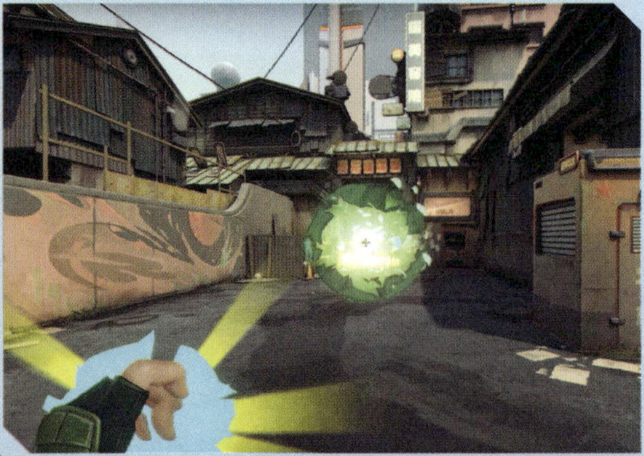

DISTRACTION

Agents such as Jett and Breach can use skills to distract the enemy team, leading them away from sites or into traps. Jett can dash and jump through an area without getting hit as easily, frustrating opponents. Breach can use his skills to blind and disorient, opening up a route for your team to swarm in.

BLOCKING

Blocking can be physical, like Sage's wall, which stops gunfire, or vision-impairing, like Brimstone's Sky Smoke. Covering a window or corridor can control where enemies will move next. With two possible entries, blocking one will allow you to set up to defend the other more aggressively.

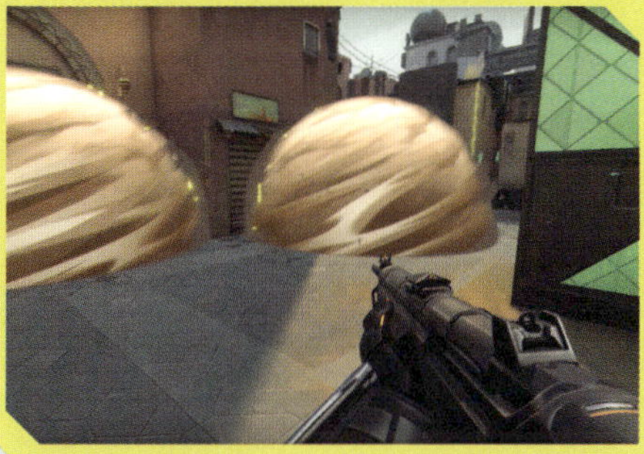

DAMAGE

Some agents are only suited to play offensively – Raze, Viper and Reyna are a few examples. Viper has an arsenal of poisons at her disposal to deplete an enemy's health, while Reyna is a one-woman wrecking ball with 'Empress' activated, shooting faster and automatically healing on a kill.

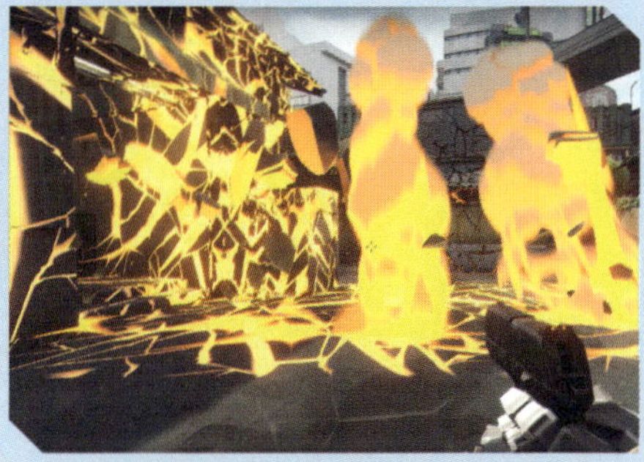

SURVEILLANCE

Cypher, Sova and Killjoy each have devices to reveal info on enemy positions. They can be destroyed in a few shots, but placed in the right areas, they can help guide the team and keep them focused on where the enemy might appear, as long as info is communicated well.

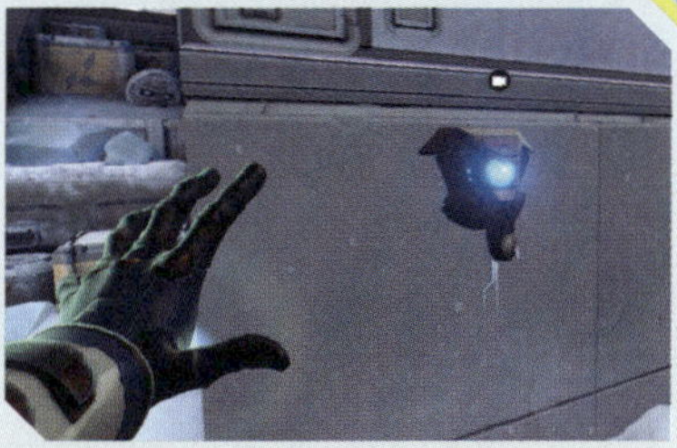

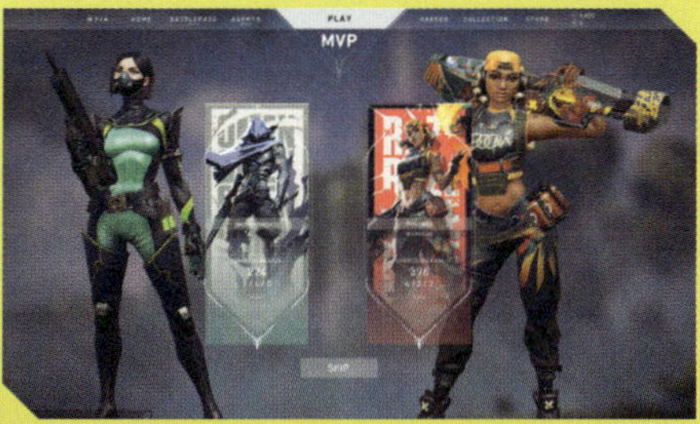

TEAM BALANCE

Before locking in an agent, consider what agent selections your team have already made. If your team is too offensive, it won't be very good at holding off a sneaky approach. Too many defensive agents, and you won't have the attacking threat to match opponents.

MOVEMENT ESSENTIALS AND GENERAL TIPS

PEEKING

Looking around walls is something you need to learn and practise to hit the top levels of Valorant. Move slightly to see around a corner, take a shot, then move back behind cover. Your crosshair should stay as close to the wall you're peeking around as possible, so when you sidestep to peek, you can take a straight, easy shot.

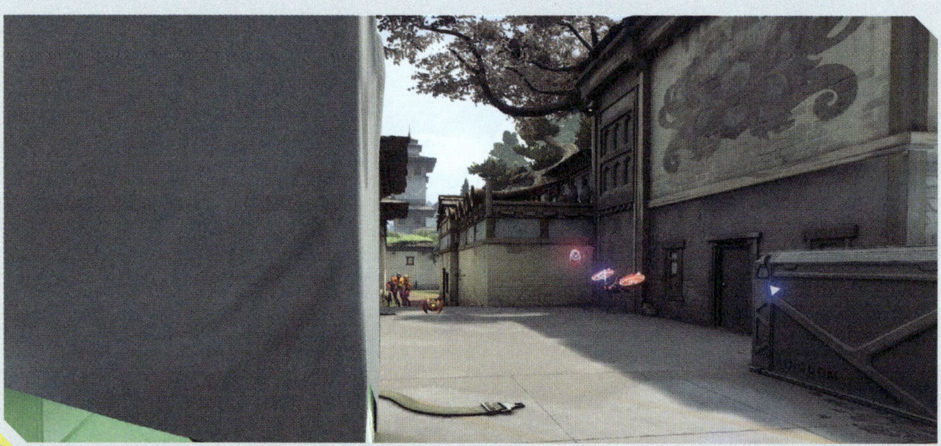

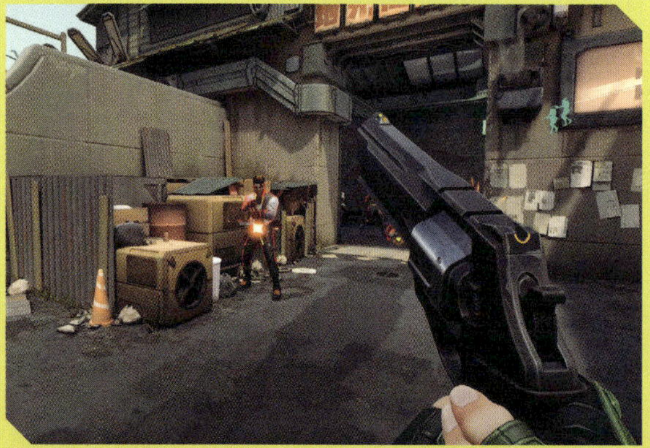

SIDESTEPPER

When waiting to shoot, move from side to side. Enemies will aim for the head, but could miss a killshot if you're dodging. The head is already a tough target, so make it even harder to get a good aim. Generally you'll have more accuracy when standing still, so move side-to-side until you see your target, then stop and take your shot.

KNIFE RUNNING

Every weapon has a different weight – basically, the bigger the gun, the heavier it is. Your movement speed is slower when carrying a gun, especially machine guns, compared to carrying a knife. It's best to equip a knife while moving to a position, then switch to a gun when you arrive to get the best of both worlds.

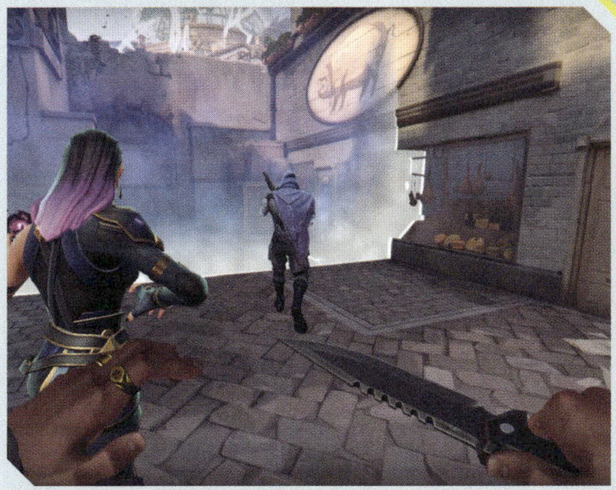

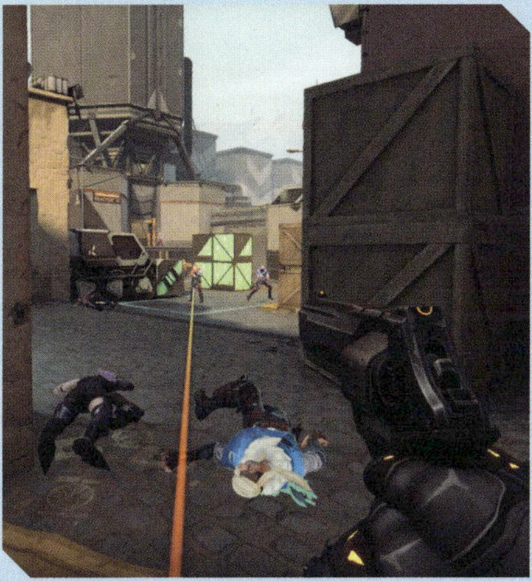

SURPRISE ATTACK

Jumping around corners can work well if you know an enemy is waiting for you. A good rule in Valorant is to hold your crosshair at head height. If you jump around the corner, not only will this confuse an enemy, but if they shoot, they're more likely to hit your body or legs rather than a fatal headshot and you have a chance to return fire.

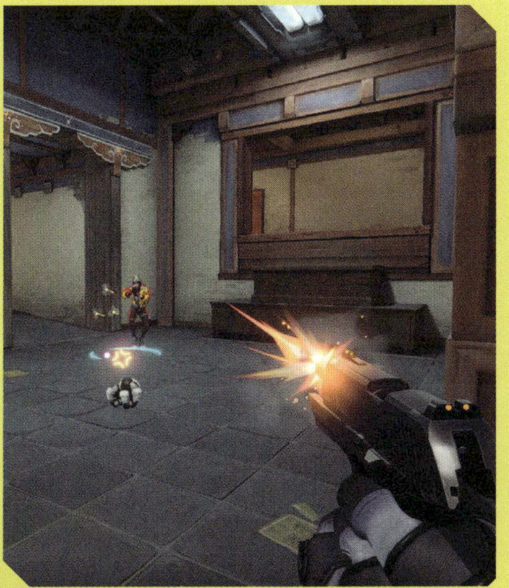

UNUSUAL PATTERNS

Your movement should always be unpredictable, whether you're under fire or not. This will throw off your enemy and make them second guess their shots, forcing them to waste ammo, or even move to a new position. Think about what's around you – is there a box you can jump onto? Why not jump and land into a crouch? Can you fall back and try new angles?

POST-GAME AND CAREER

Once a match ends, you'll see a post-game summary about the performance of both teams. From the Career tab in the main menu, you can view the summaries for your last dozen games. It's bursting with stats and highlights how well you've performed against individuals, or where you can improve.

CAREER OVERVIEW

Your Career tab opens on your overview, which shows your Act Rank on the left and your season rank card, which is filled as you win Ranked matches. On the right-hand side of the screen, you'll see a list of your recent matches and a snapshot of info about each of them.

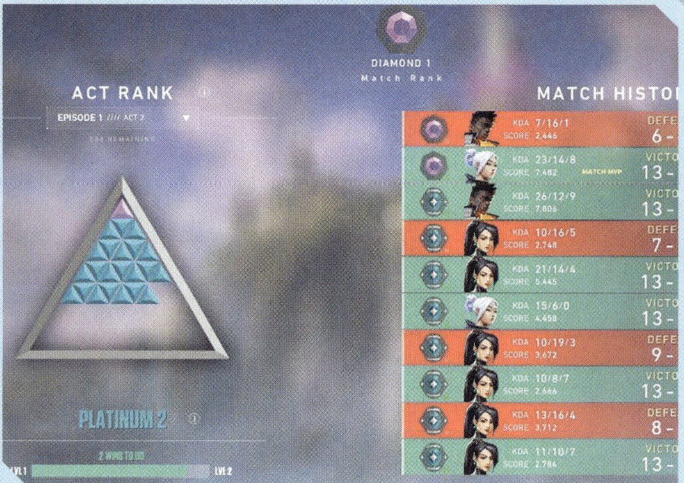

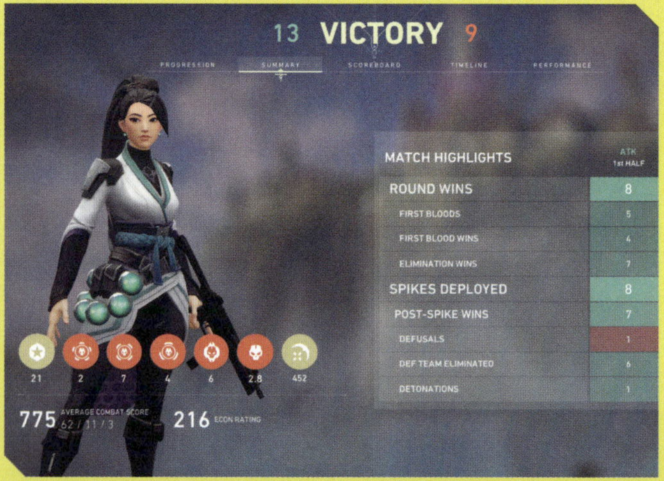

MATCH SUMMARY

Clicking one of the matches will bring up a summary with multiple tabs. The first tab shows you all the details about your performance – your combat score, average kills per round, first bloods and much more. It'll also have details on the match, including the score.

SCOREBOARD

The scoreboard tab shows how each player performed in different aspects, including combat score, econ rating (how well you did versus the money you spent) and KDAs. The standings are ranked on 'Average Combat Score' by default but can be reorganised by clicking on each of the headings. It's great to see how well you played compared to others on your team.

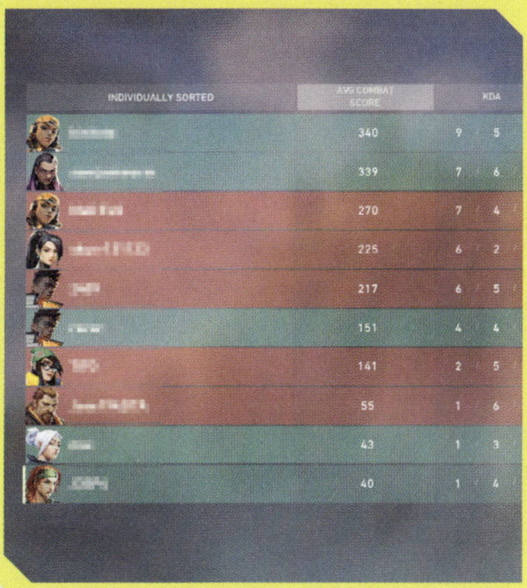

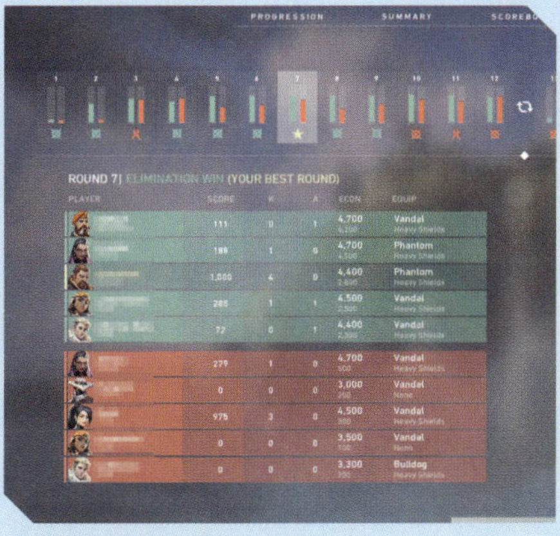

TIMELINE

In the timeline tab, you'll see a breakdown of the kills in every round, from the weapon that landed the finishing blow and when an agent was eliminated, to the location of the death on the map. You can switch between every round to see how it was won – whether the spike exploded, was defused, or a team wiped out – and see how you performed in each, including how money was spent, and everyone's individual combat score.

PERFORMANCE

The last tab shows how you played against each enemy, how many times you killed them and how many times they got the better of you. A silver star by the enemy agent's row means you did surprisingly well against the agent – a gold one means you exceeded expectations. Click on each agent to see details of the times you killed, assisted or died against that particular enemy.

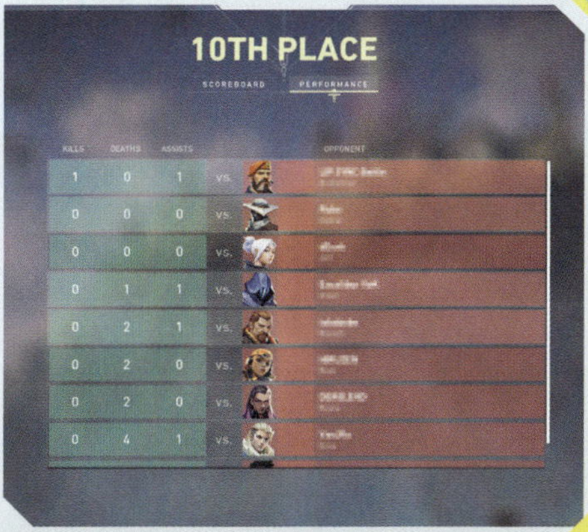

BATTLE PASS

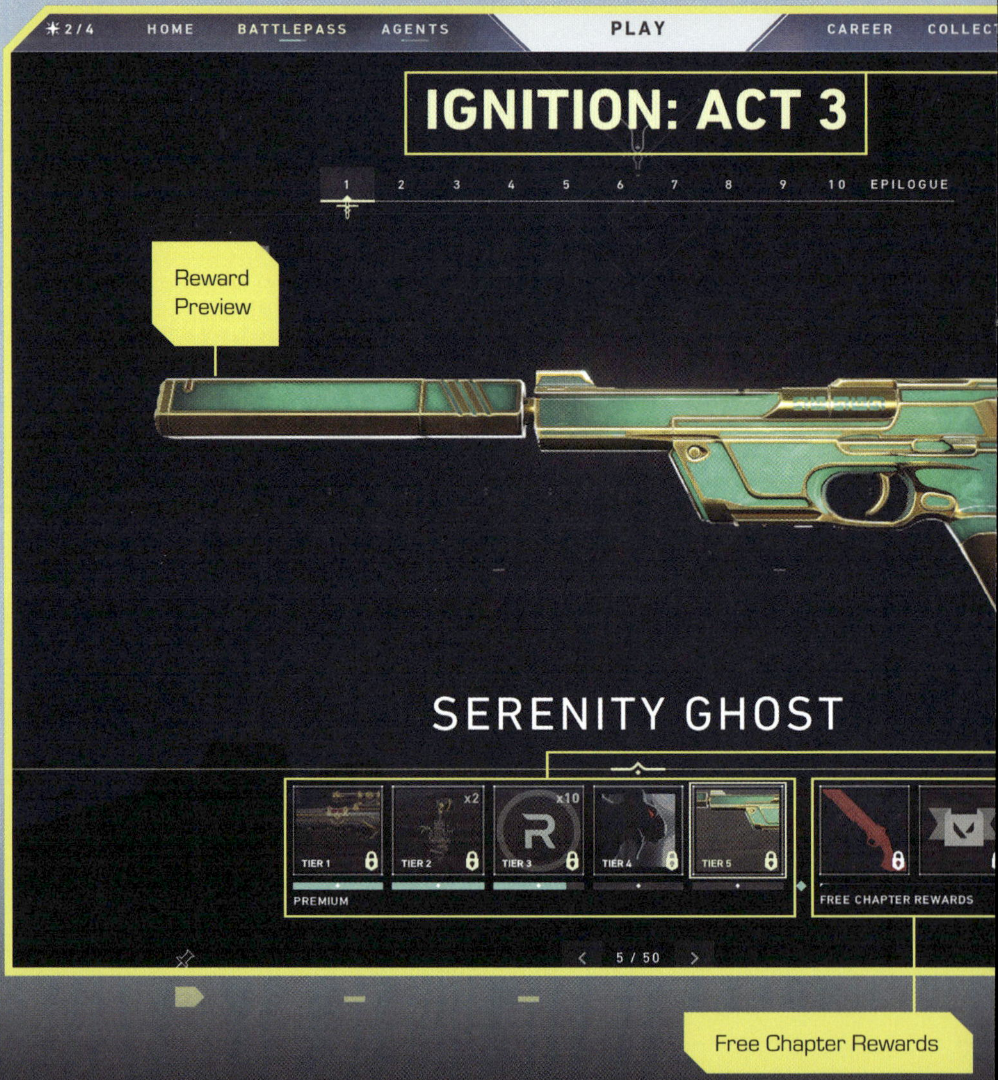
2/4
HOME
BATTLEPASS
AGENTS
PLAY
CAREER
IGNITION: ACT 3
1 2 3 4 5 6 7 8 9 10 EPILOGUE
Reward Preview
SERENITY GHOST
TIER 1
TIER 2
TIER 3
TIER 4
TIER 5
PREMIUM
FREE CHAPTER REWARDS
5 / 50
Free Chapter Rewards

The Valorant battle pass works much like others you may have seen – it defines the season by offering players the chance to work through 50 levels, which are unlocked by earning XP. For each level you will receive a reward, which might be a weapon skin, a 'buddy' to attach to your favourite gun or a new card to change your player profile.

The first era of the game was named 'Ignition' and contained three acts. These acts highlight a break in the ongoing fight and story of Valorant and a new battle pass was released with each act.

Daily and weekly missions come in different varieties and difficulties. One that rewards a small amount of XP might be to kill one enemy with an opponent's gun, while another will task you with landing 50 headshots and reward you with huge amounts of XP. Most of them can be completed fairly easily by playing a couple of games a day, so treat them as a bonus.

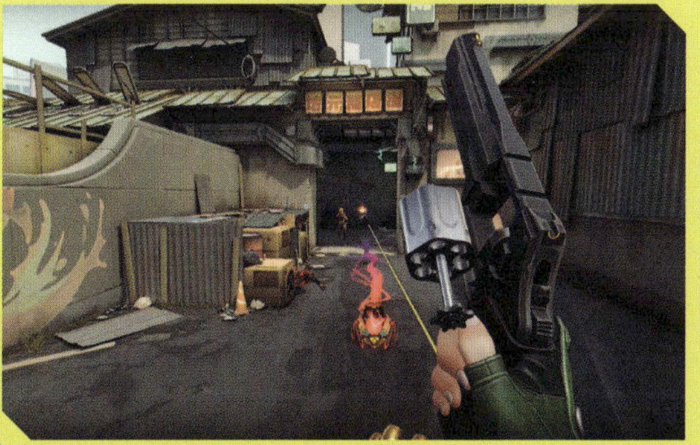

Each battle pass is broken down into tiers, and each tier you reach will unlock a new reward when you've earned enough XP. Players who don't purchase the battle pass can still complete these chapters but will only earn a reward every five tiers.

MODES AND MAPS

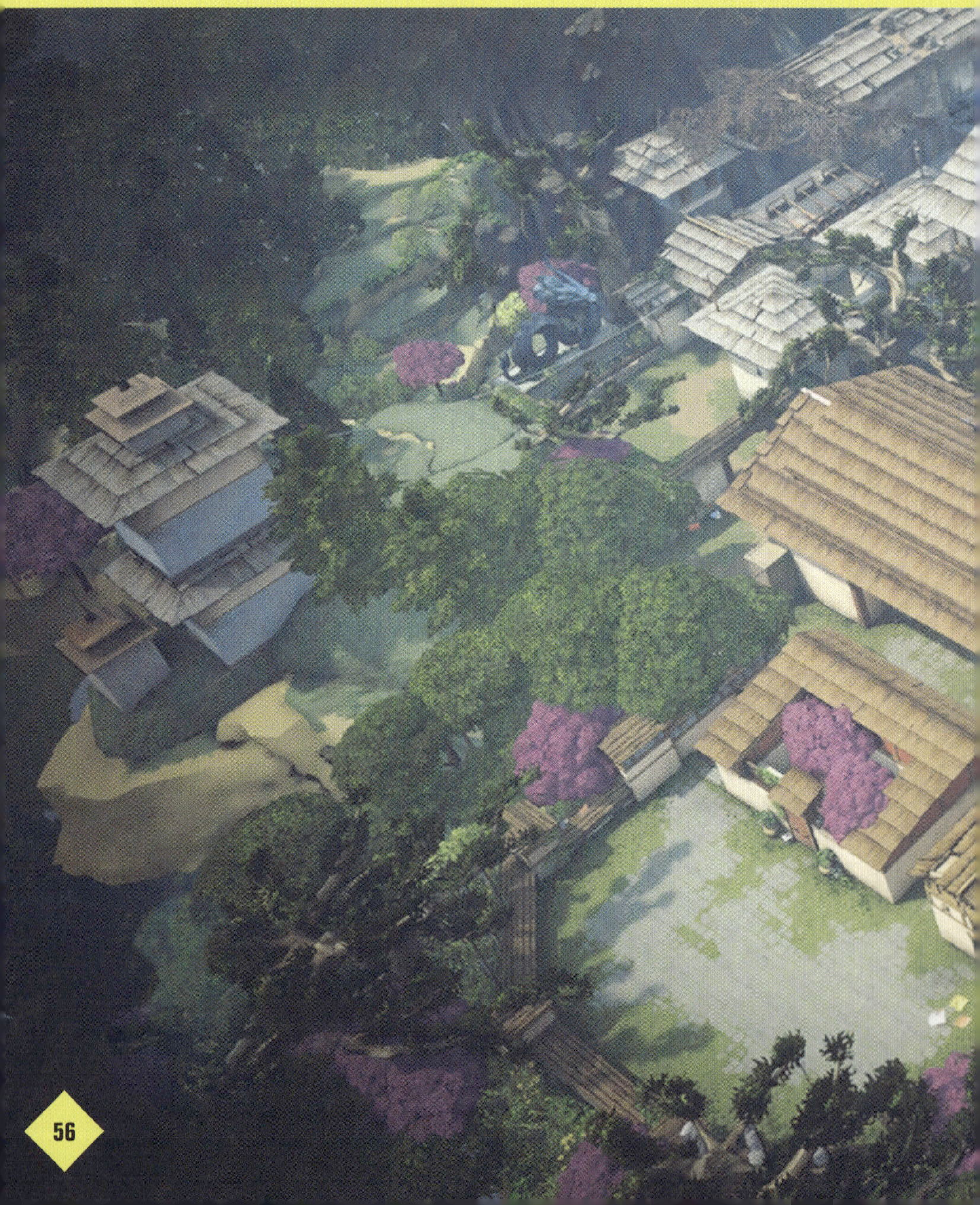

We're sure you've already jumped headfirst into the world of Valorant, but this next section will give you everything you need to master the different game modes and make the most of the several battlefields you'll drop into. From Italy's Ascent to the snow-covered Tundra in Russia, you'll gain all the tips, tricks and tactics you'll need to grab the victory, no matter where you're battling.

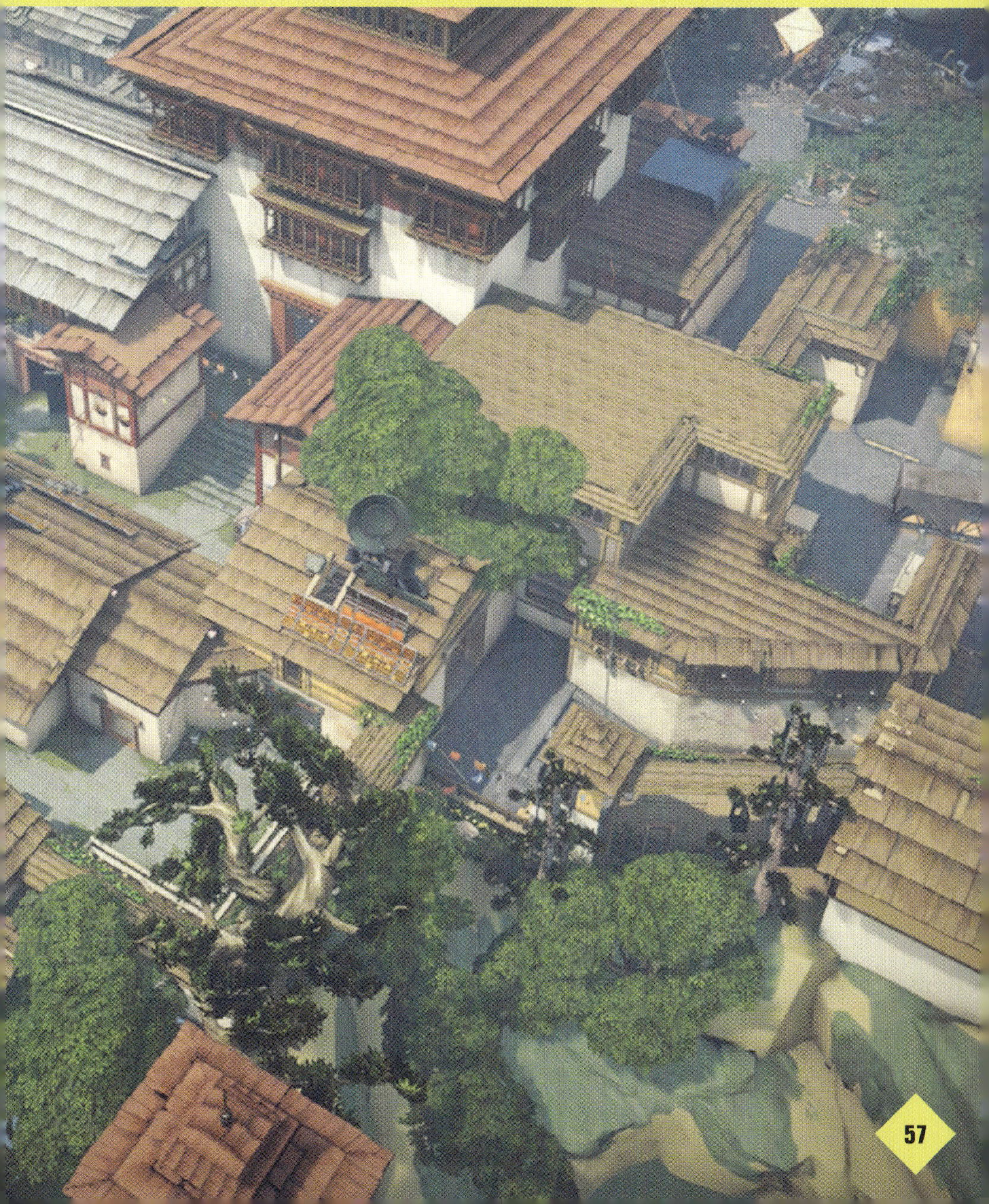

RANKED/UNRANKED

The main game mode is 'search and destroy' which has been a fixture of shooters for decades. It's the central mode, on which the whole cast of characters and story hangs on. It's a tense, action-packed game of defence and attack that is as much about tactics as it is about pure skill.

The Rules

1. Each team is made up of five agents.
2. One team starts on defence while the other attacks by carrying the spike into the defending team's half of the map.
3. The spike can only be carried by one player, but it can be passed to another member of the team.
4. Once the spike is planted, the attackers have 45 seconds to defend the site before it detonates, winning them the round.
5. Attackers also win if defenders are eliminated. Defenders win if they prevent an explosion and avoid death.
6. Each match can last up to 25 rounds. The first team to hit 13 winning rounds, wins the match.
7. If scores are tied at 12-12, the match goes into two-round overtime periods, which repeat until a team wins both rounds, or both teams call a draw.

RANKED

Ranked and Unranked are pretty much the same game; the only difference is that Ranked is a competitive section of the game where those who strive to be the best in the world will battle it out. The more wins, kills and spike interactions you have, the better you are and the higher your rank will be.

It's here that players will bring their A-game and employ their best tactics to get the win. You may even run into the occasional streamer or pro player!

The ranks are as follows, and all but the highest rank have three tiers within it:

- IRON
- BRONZE
- SILVER
- GOLD
- PLATINUM
- DIAMOND
- IMMORTAL
- RADIANT

Valorant, like many other games, uses a season system; referred to in-game as 'Acts'. An act generally lasts around two months – you can play Ranked matches to increase your skill and earn the highest tier possible. Once the act ends, rankings will be reset, ready for the next act to start.

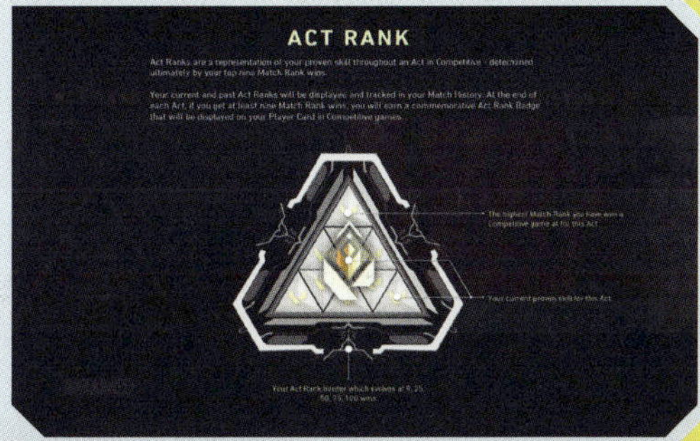

SPIKE RUSH

Spike Rush is a frantic mode that is over much quicker than the main Ranked and Unranked modes! It was designed for those players who want to jump straight into the action and not worry too much about the patient tactical element.

What Are The Differences?

1. A game of Spike Rush generally lasts around 8-12 minutes.
2. Every attacking player has a spike to plant and detonate, so agents can swarm the sites to gain points.
3. There are only seven total rounds in Spike Rush, attacking and defending teams swap over after just three rounds.
4. Players start with random weapons. One round you may be given a shotgun, and the next you could have a sniper rifle.
5. All basic abilities are refreshed every round, so no need to monitor how many you are using during a battle.
6. With every kill or death, you are given two ultimate points. This means if you play well ... or even really badly, you can unleash your ultimate ability pretty often. We did say it was chaotic.
7. Each round, several powerup orbs will spawn on the map.

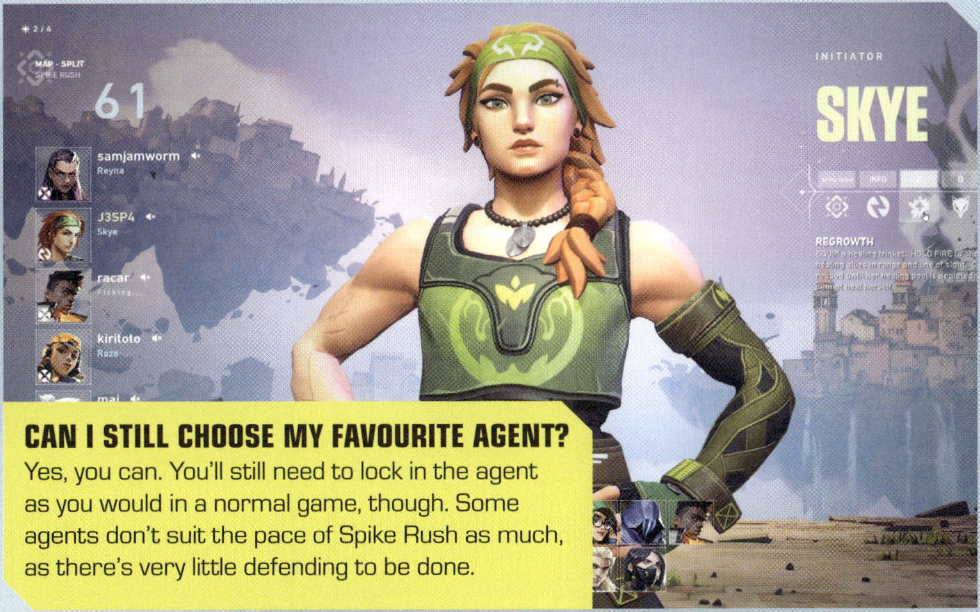

CAN I STILL CHOOSE MY FAVOURITE AGENT?

Yes, you can. You'll still need to lock in the agent as you would in a normal game, though. Some agents don't suit the pace of Spike Rush as much, as there's very little defending to be done.

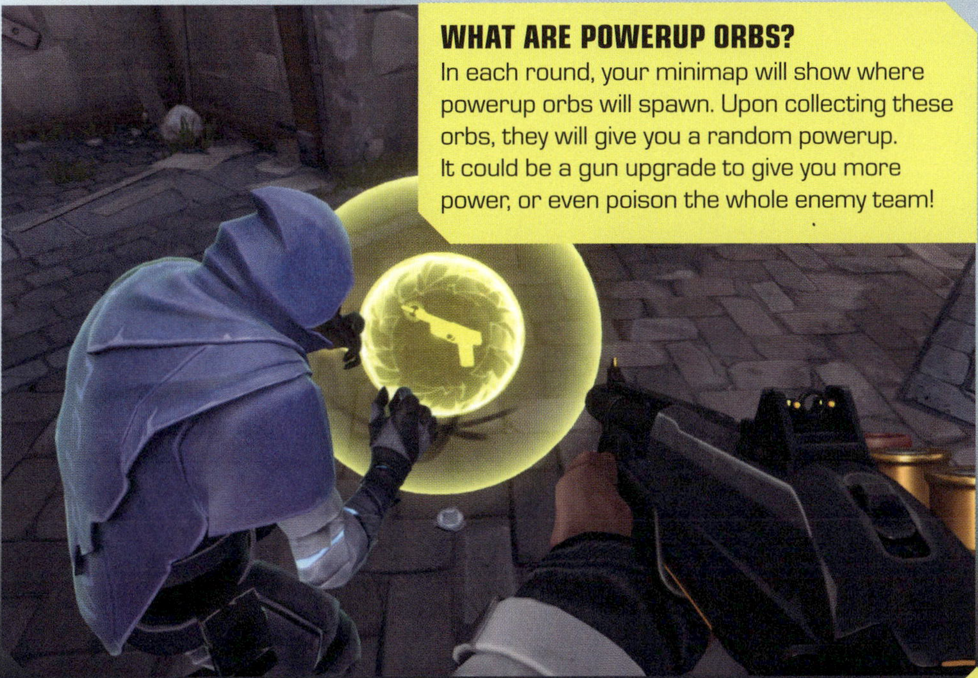

WHAT ARE POWERUP ORBS?

In each round, your minimap will show where powerup orbs will spawn. Upon collecting these orbs, they will give you a random powerup. It could be a gun upgrade to give you more power, or even poison the whole enemy team!

SPIKE RUSH TACTICS

Rush is a very different style of match to the usual Valorant games you'll play. Everything is built around fast-paced action and random moments. This comes from the ability to plant spikes at any point, weapons rotating in and out with each round and powerup orbs dotted around the map which change the outcome every time. Getting used to Spike Rush can be tricky but by keeping some basics in mind, you'll have lots of fun while hopefully scoring some wins.

RANDOM WEAPONS

Spend some time getting familiar with every weapon before entering Spike Rush. You will be given a random weapon in each round and you will need to adapt to it. Learn how each gun recoils when fired, how long it takes to reload, how slow you are when moving, and if you can Aim Down Sights (ADS) with it and still move. This is something that will help you improve in all modes, but you can also watch your teammates to see how they use different weapons too.

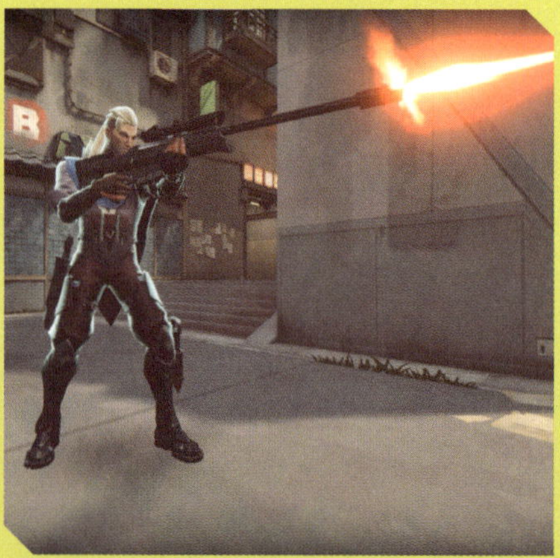

ALL-OUT ATTACK

You cannot play defensively in Spike Rush! Every attacker has a spike and is trying to reach the plant sites. Those powerup orbs will be taken if you're sat back watching an angle. Try to keep moving, grab the orbs quickly and don't give enemies a moment's peace. This goes for attacking too. Creeping around isn't going to score you points. That spike needs to get to the right place. Pushing with your team will help.

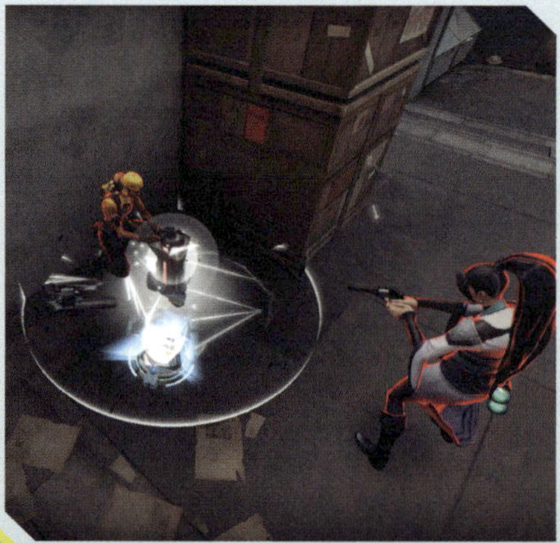

ORBS

Powerup orbs can turn the tide of any Spike Rush game. They have the ability of turning a losing team into a winning one, if you know which to use and when. Picking these up needs to become second nature; they show up on the main and mini maps, you'll need to be aware that others might be heading to the same orb as you.

Remember, they take a few seconds to collect, so stay on your toes for a fight.

INSTANT ULTIMATE

Exactly as it sounds, this orb gives you an ultimate ability to use immediately.

HEALTH ORB

This orb doesn't just heal you, but the whole team, for 12 points per second.

DECEPTION ORB

3 seconds after grabbing this orb, your opponent's vision will shrink, they will start to hear false footsteps and gunshots, confusing them completely! This effect lasts for 10 seconds.

DAMAGE AMP

Grabbing this orb will boost the damage of your current gun until the end of the round.

HYPER SPEED

You and any nearby allies will receive a speed boost if you collect this orb.

CRIPPLING DECAY

After 2.5 seconds everyone on the enemy team will only have 10 points of health. When it wears off, their health will be restored.

GOLDEN GUN

This gives you a gun that 'one-taps' enemies, plus it's as light as a knife. It only has one bullet though, which is restored if you kill an enemy.

WEAPON UPGRADE

Want a better gun? Grab this orb. It will give you a more powerful weapon.

DEATHMATCH

Don't want to play as a team for a while? Fancy leaving the spike at home, while you rampage through the maps fragging everyone in sight? Deathmatch is your answer.

Deathmatch is a free-for-all mode where there are no teams, no abilities, no spikes or sites and plenty of money to buy whatever weapon you want. Deathmatch is still played on the familiar maps and you still choose an agent – though this is just cosmetic – but the idea is to grab as many eliminations as possible to win the game. The first person to reach 30 kills is the winner!

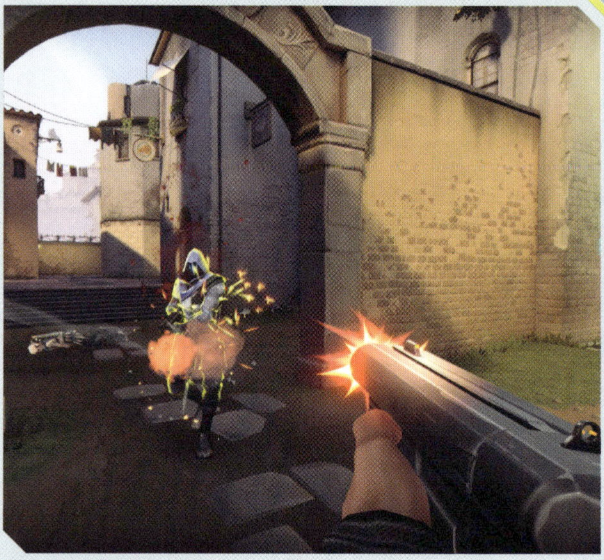

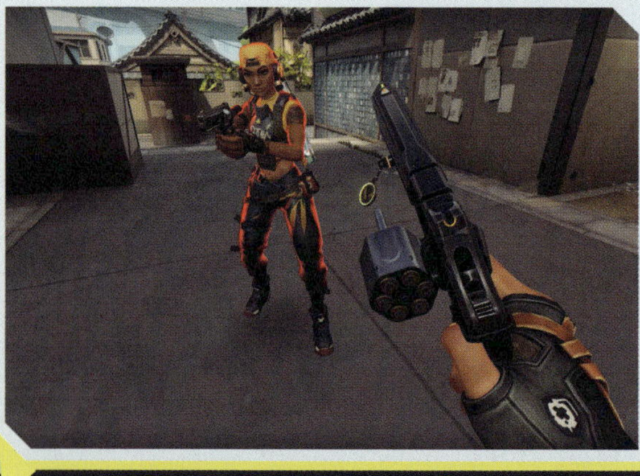

For a while, many players were asking for a proper way to practise the game without jeopardising their rank. There's only so much you can get out of the shooting range or the use of AI bots. So, Deathmatch can be used as a practice area for you to test out new weapons or even new tactics to move through the maps.

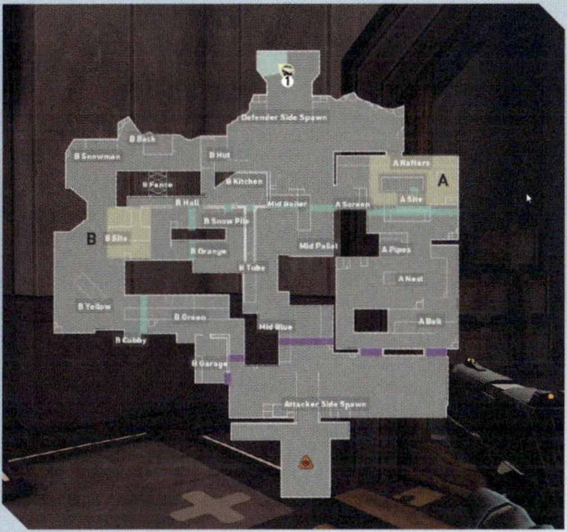

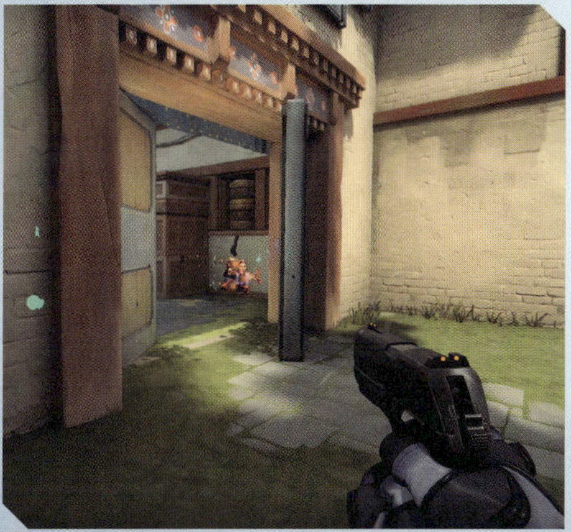

HELPFUL HINTS

- When an enemy is eliminated, they drop health and ammo. Picking these up will reload your weapon, meaning you won't need to pause your rampage, you can concentrate on racking up the score.
- The minimap refreshes every five seconds to show enemy positions. They'll move between those updates, but it helps you gauge where the action is.
- Use this mode to practise your gunplay basics – crouch-shooting and keeping your crosshair at head height on corners.
- As with other modes, you will earn XP in Deathmatch, but it's very low compared to Spike Rush and the standard modes.
- No need to earn credits here, you have unlimited money available, so choose whichever weapons you want.

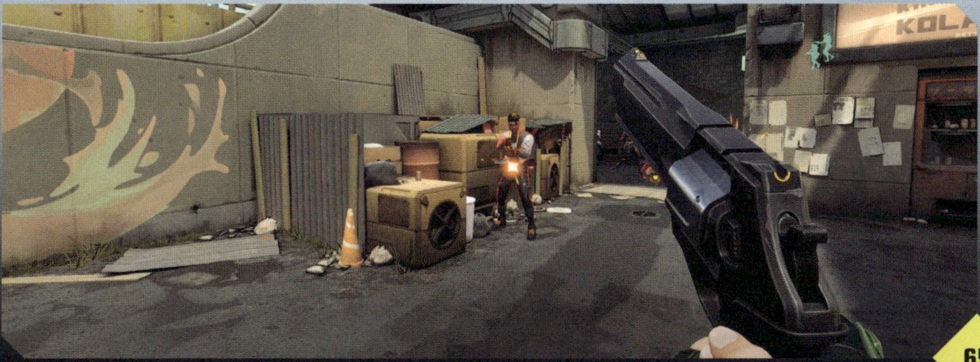

CUSTOM GAMES

The ability to set up a custom game may be a bit of an unknown for some players. This is an area of the game most commonly used in tournaments and pro league games, but it's also a handy place to get your friends together and play a game exactly how you might want. Over these two pages we'll explain everything you might need to know for setting up a custom game.

MAP

From this drop-down menu you will be able to select the map where your custom game will be played – Haven, Bind, Ascent, Split or Icebox.

MAP: Ascent
Ascent
Split
Bind
Icebox
Haven

MODE

Here you will choose from the standard game modes and set out the rules you want to use; Standard, Spike Rush or Deathmatch. Note that choosing Deathmatch will eliminate the need for teams.

MODE: Standard
Standard
Deathmatch
Spike Rush

SERVER

This one is particularly important. You will want to choose a server which is central to you and your friends. For example, if you're all playing in the UK, then you'll choose a server based either in the UK, or as close as possible. This means that all your PCs will communicate with the server in less time, cutting down on lag and slower input times from your button presses.

SERVER: London ▼
Frankfurt 2
Paris 2
Warsaw
Bahrain
Frankfurt 1
Paris 1

OPTIONS

In options you will have three toggles to change aspects of the game. You can apply cheats, which makes the game play differently – maybe more chaotic or you might agree to a sniper-only game. You can play with tournament mode switched on, which creates a sense of playing in a league. Finally, you can change the overtime rule, which kicks in if the game ends in a draw.

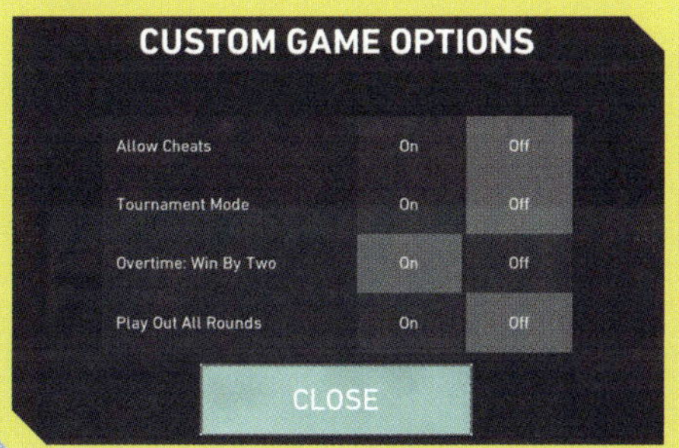

SPECTATORS

This option is mainly used for pro games, where individual referees need to be present in the match. Anybody added here cannot be seen within the map and they can't interfere with the match. They're only there to ensure everyone plays fair and there is no cheating or communicating between teams.

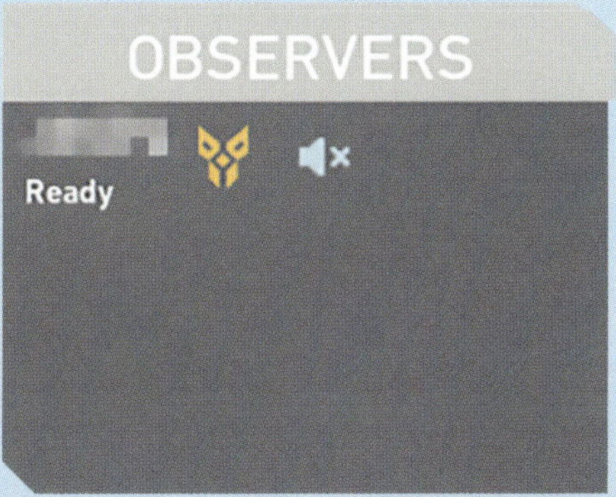

TEAMS

Now it's time to assign teams. You can freely move people from side to side if you want to see how some players will play against a group of others.

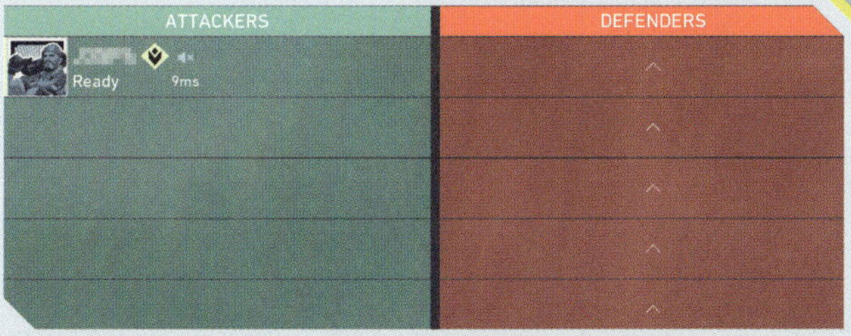

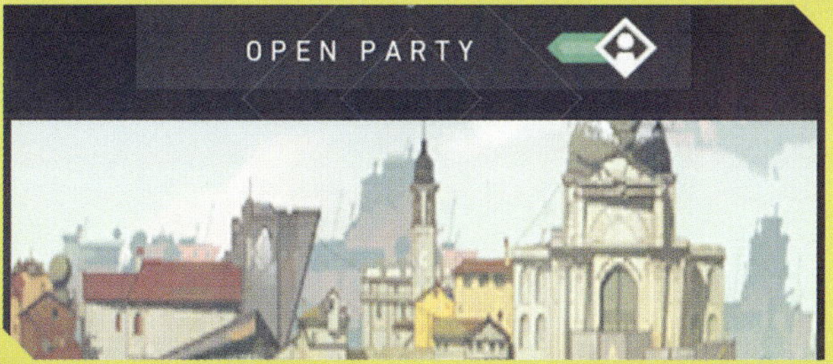

OPEN/CLOSE

Lastly you can set the game to open or closed. If you toggle an open game, anyone will be able to join. Whereas choosing closed means that only those invited can play in your custom game.

ASCENT

Ascent features many large open areas for team brawls, and plenty of long corridors that are ideal for snipers. This European-style map sees plenty of frantic action, among the cafés, archways and rustic bridges. With large, closable blast doors, Ascent offers a challenge for both attackers and defenders as they try to find new routes through this extra layer of security.

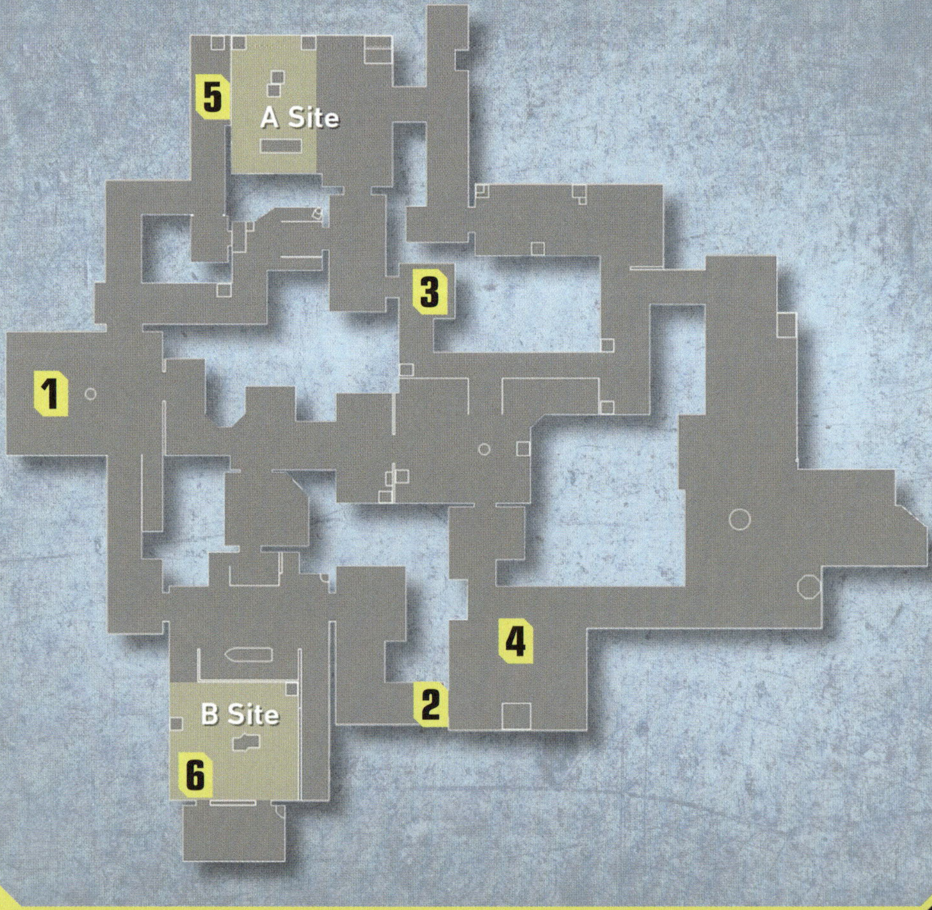

LOCATION TIPS

1 It's a short trip for defenders to cover either of the sites in Ascent. If you find yourself covering A Site and notice B is under attack, you can rotate very quickly. Be on your guard and be ready to sprint to the other site.

2 Remember, the blast doors can be shot and broken down. With enough firepower you could distract the defenders into thinking you're wrapping around the area, when really you're prepping to destroy the doors.

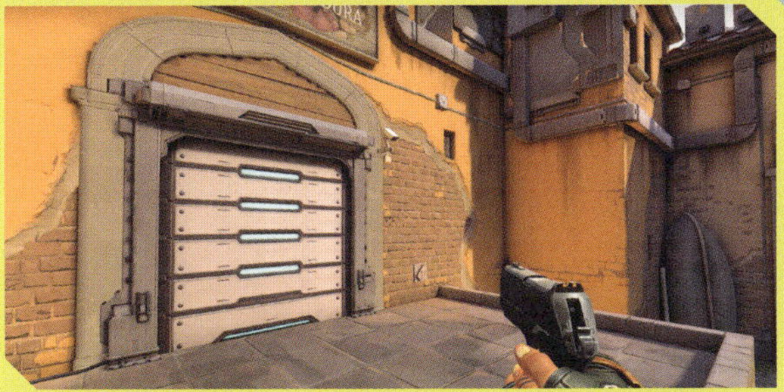

3 It's very easy to get caught up in the middle areas as there's little space to move here and lots of places to get stuck. Avoid getting pinned down here, or you'll be easy pickings for the enemy team.

4 You only have one route to B Site from B Lobby, whereas defenders can push the same route and flank from Mid. You'll need to be fast if you want to get in and establish a line of sight.

5 Defending from A Rafters is the most obvious call, and you might get off a few shots before the attackers look up. The issue is, they can easily block your vision from there, so you're best off ordering a couple of teammates to hide behind the boxes so someone can always keep an eye on the entrance.

6 The best defence for B Site is to hug the bottom wall and set up in the corner near the back. This gives a great vantage for seeing attackers, but it does leave you open, so make sure you have someone else watching your angles or laying down cover fire.

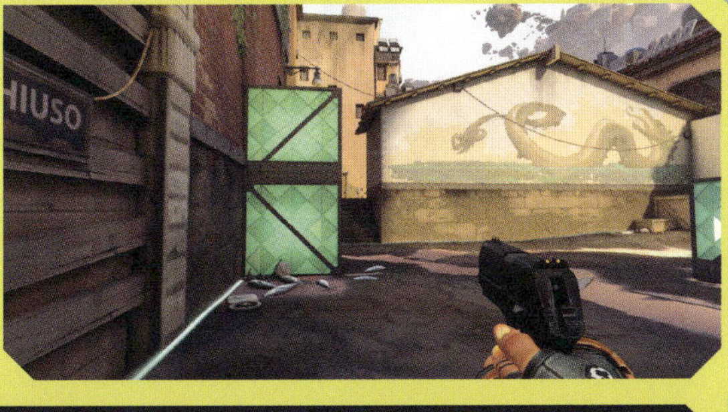

BIND

Bind is a collection of small areas, set within an unnamed town in the Middle East, where the sand is an all-consuming force. Cave systems and ramped inclines frame the map, offering brief rest from the ongoing fighting. Bind doesn't feature many long, narrow corridors; most of the sites nudge up against one another, with occasional wide hallways.

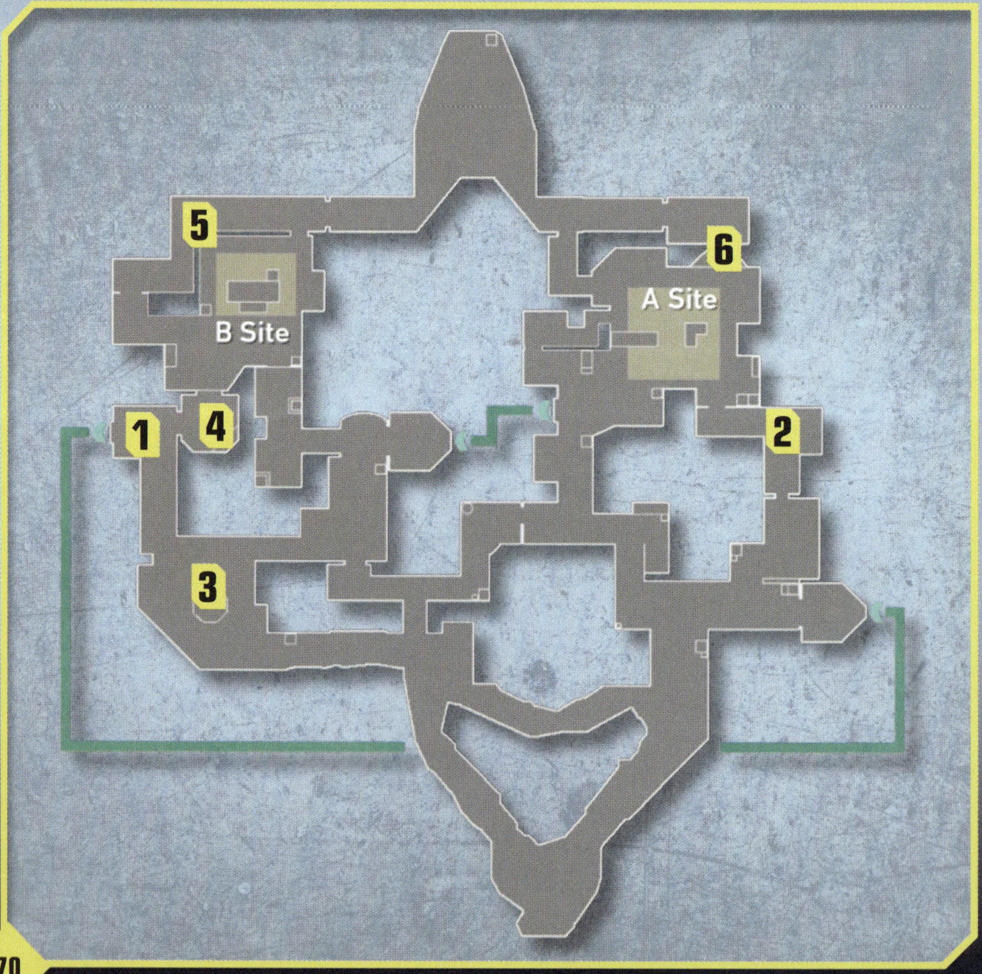

LOCATION TIPS

1 Teleporters are unique to Bind and provide fast movement around the map. If you're attacking, be aware of camping enemies when exiting. If defending, listen out for the unique sound it makes and watch out for an extra enemy.

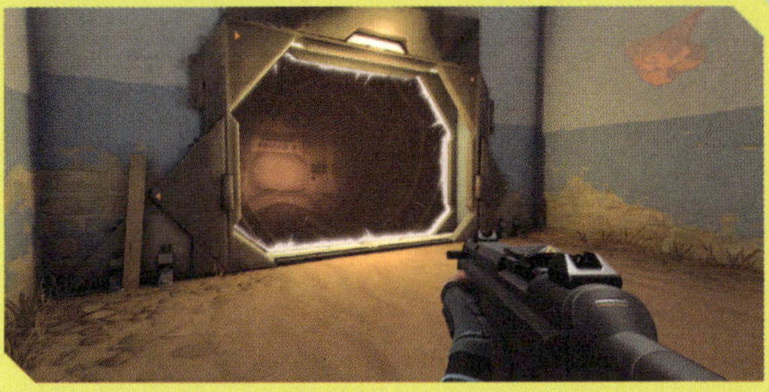

2 Any attackers heading to A could enter through A Bath. You can set up traps, but also be aware of sightlines. You can stand guard from A Bath and keep an eye on anyone coming out of the teleporter.

3 The fountain near B is a hard area to pass through as it connects to two corridors with easy sightlines. Hide progress through this area with abilities such as Brimstone's smoke or Viper's Poison Cloud.

4 B Garden is often overlooked as an entry point, but only at a defender's peril. There are spots on site where you can watch B Garden and B Long, as well as anyone escaping to the teleporter.

5 Besides the obvious routes directly to B site, B Elbow can provide a surprising way of reaching the site. If one or more of your team can reach this corner, either from A Site or by sneaking from B Garden, you can surprise defenders from behind and make it easier for others to get on site.

6 A Tower has the best viewing point from which to defend A Site. Your team should always have someone stationed here, as you can see all three entrances to the site. Cypher is preferable as he can set up his camera to spy even further afield and keep the site on lockdown.

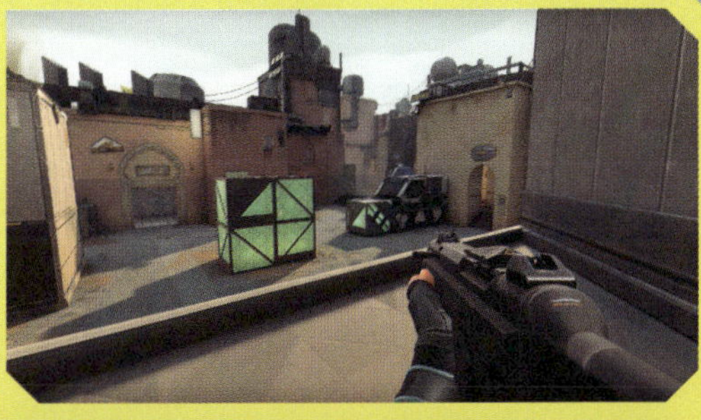

HAVEN

Haven, much like Bind, is a series of interconnecting rooms with very few corridors. The centre of this temple-based map has a wide-open space that requires sharp eyes from defenders. Leftover stacks of bricks and sandbags offer small pockets of cover in an otherwise quite empty and open area. It has more ground to cover and an extra site to attack or defend.

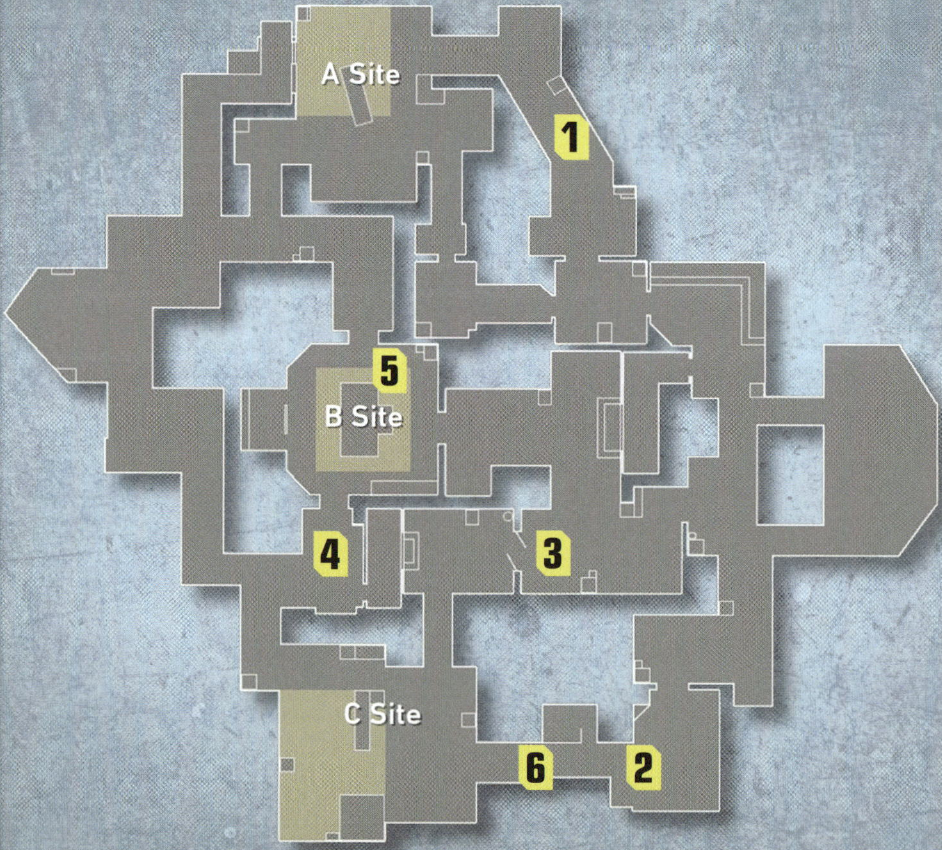

LOCATION TIPS

1 Attacking on Haven can be a little tougher than on other maps. A Long is a popular route to site, but a defending wall from Sage is enough to slow attackers and pick them off as the wall is broken.

2 If you want to get sniped, C Long is where it will happen. You'll need to smoke the entrance to avoid being picked off quickly, but you could end up being flanked by defenders as soon as you enter site too.

3 The double doors at Mid will likely see some action. Use the doors to your advantage. Smoke them if wanting to pass through, but if you're keeping guard, destroy the door coverings so you can achieve some penetration damage too.

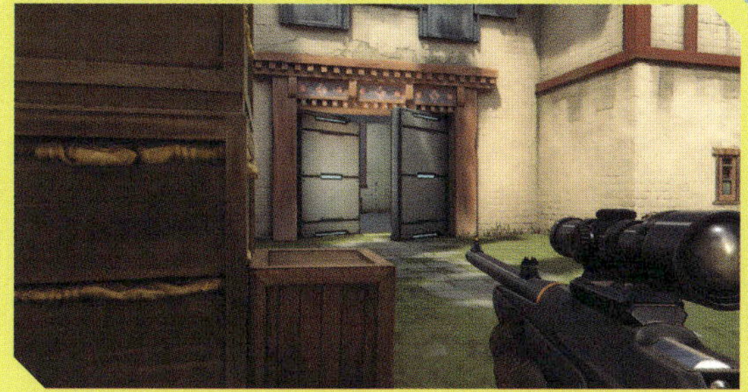

4 At first glance, B Site looks easy to attack, but the boxes in the middle actually make things a lot harder. There are lots of nooks for defenders to sit in and keep watch. You have to move into B Site as if it was full of players – check your angles, clears your corners and sweep the room before planting the spike.

5 B Site can often get quite chaotic; it's a small room with lots of tight angles and cover points. Hold your corners and make sure you're listening for footsteps. Often your ears are better for defence than your eyes – flicking your camera around means missing movement that your ears will catch easily.

6 Time for your sniper to take the stage. Whoever on your team is strongest at sniping, get them to C Long and the cubby halfway down it. Here they can watch over C Site as the rest of the team moves through the double doors, which should allow your team to surround defenders.

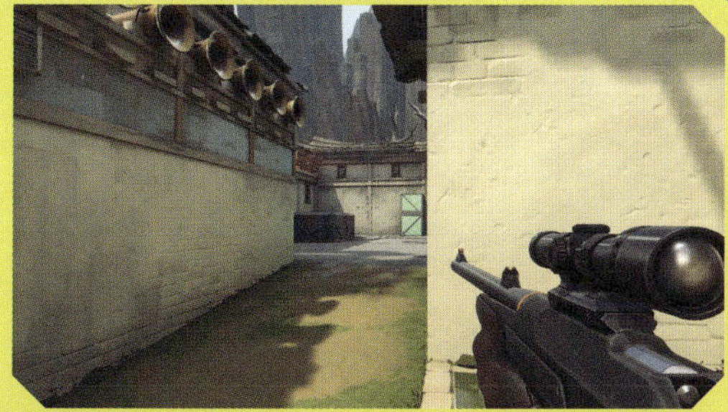

ICEBOX

Dug out of the ice by Kingdom, Icebox is a frosty map which was swallowed by the tundra. There are two plant sites to the map, but it's a rat's nest of corridors and interior areas. Compared to the other maps, Icebox is cluttered with corners to hide behind for cover. However, there are plenty of sight lines to take advantage of and ziplines to help you to traverse the area quickly.

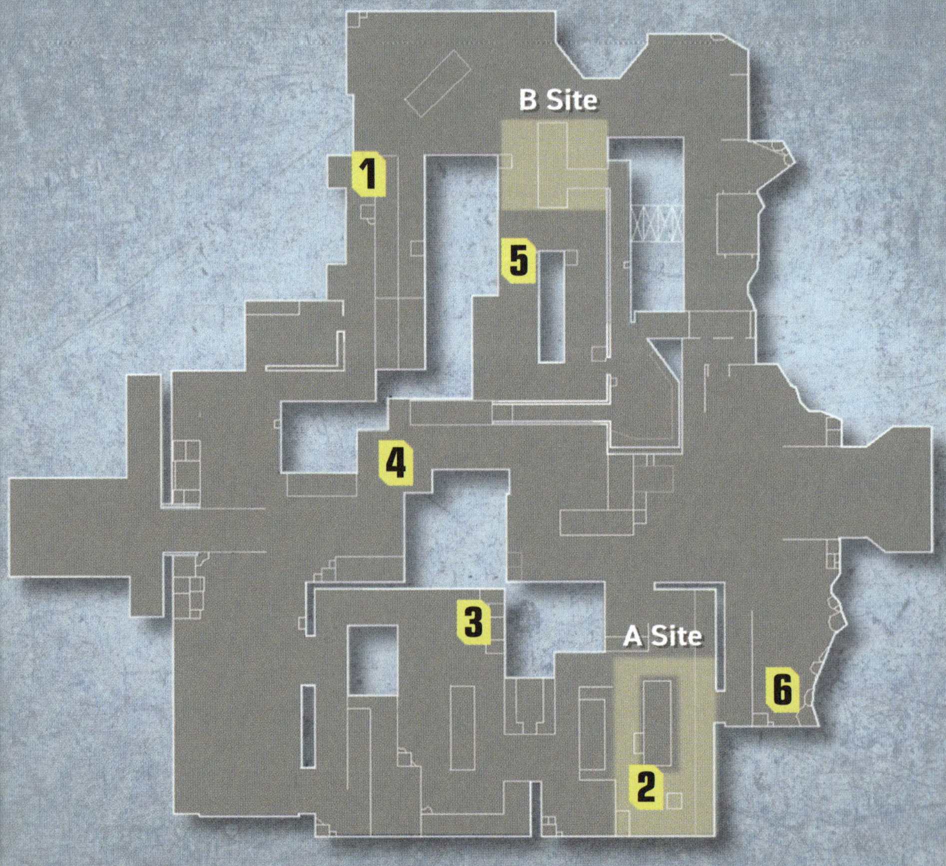

LOCATION TIPS

1 Placing a sniper in, or close to, this cubby near B will give you good coverage of the right side of the map. While you're not pushing the site, it does mean you can cover the spike carrier or lie in wait for an ambush.

2 A Site has a couple of ziplines that make it easy to zoom straight onto your objective. However, there are a lot of walls for defenders to hide behind, so attackers should peek just as carefully on the zipline as on foot.

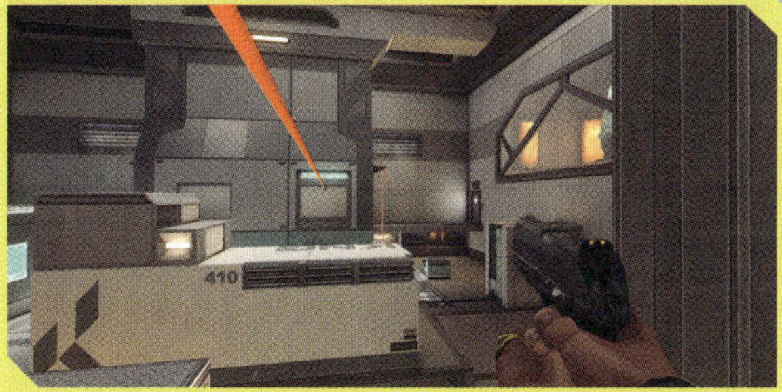

3 There's always an elevated point to watch or snipe from but hiding up in the rafters in A will leave you too open. It's an obvious place to cover from, so wait until late in the round before rotating up there.

4 This central area of the map is a choke point; anyone attacking through here can be held back easily. If you rush it as a team, using flashes and disruption abilities, you may squeak through.

5 Rather than pushing to the sides, consider moving through Mid and splitting off to B Site. It will be harder to defend as it's closed-in.

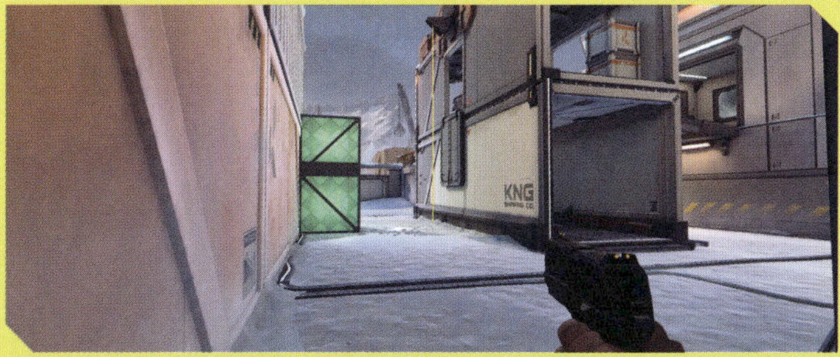

6 This top corner of A Site has nice sightlines to keep watch on your spike planter. You can watch from behind two separate boxes here to help with cover.

SPLIT

Towers, zip-ropes and lots of vertical vantages come together to make Split one of the more interesting maps for movement. Set in the futuristic slums of South America, Split is a home for fringe technology as it creeps in to rule everyday life. With lots of winding alleyways and two spike sites split far apart, you'll face tough choices whether you're attacking or defending.

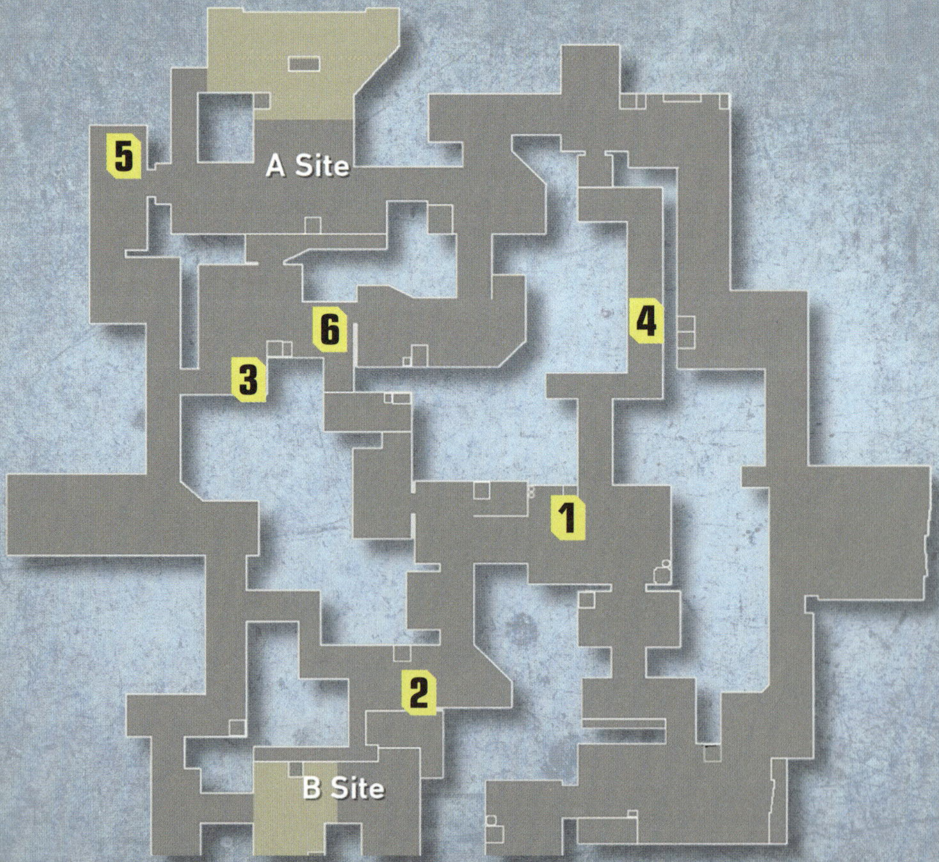

LOCATION TIPS

1 With such a wide middle ground between the two sites, the initial choice of pushing A or B is a tough one. Try to work and stay together, if you split up you will lose the round.

2 The ropes are a great feature of Split and help to gain height to watch over areas. However, they're noisy and you're an unarmed target while using them. Choose when to move wisely and avoid these deaths.

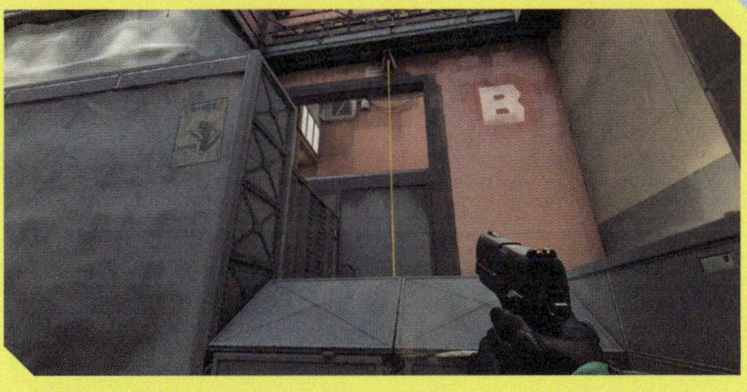

3 These towers are helpful to gain height advantage and keep watch, but don't camp in them without someone covering your back. Attackers can hold down the spike if they can turn these spots over.

4 A Sewer is a well-trodden path for attackers. Many players will think they're being crafty by using the sewers to move, but listen for water splashing if you're nearby as it's a dead giveaway!

5 Defending A Site can be done from two points – the cubby at the back of A Long or from A Ramps. If the attacking team choose A, they only have one main point of entry and a defending team set up on either of these points will have a clear advantage as they pass through the choke point.

6 When attacking, try to avoid the obvious entry along A Main as much as possible. Use A Ramps to get into A Tower, which will at least give you more corners and cover to hide behind.

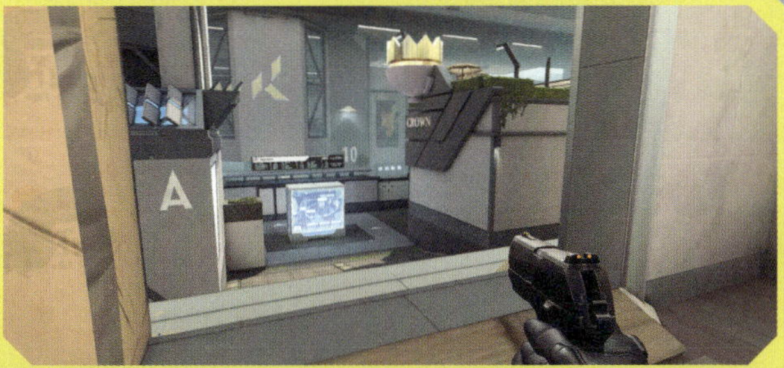

GOODBYE

So, there we have it. Hopefully, you're on your way to becoming Radiant. It's been quite a journey; from breaking down the weapons, meeting the agents at your disposal and travelling the world via the impressive maps, you should be quite the Valorant expert by now.

Valorant is already such an exciting game, but with every act that passes, there are important changes, new challenges and cool additional characters and maps. It's always evolving and you'll need to keep your skills sharp to reach the top.

The most important thing is that you're having fun, staying safe and being kind to other players. Remember that winning is only part of playing Valorant; support other members of the community, play fair and keep calm under pressure. Enjoy the game and have fun!

We'll see you on the battlefield, Agent!

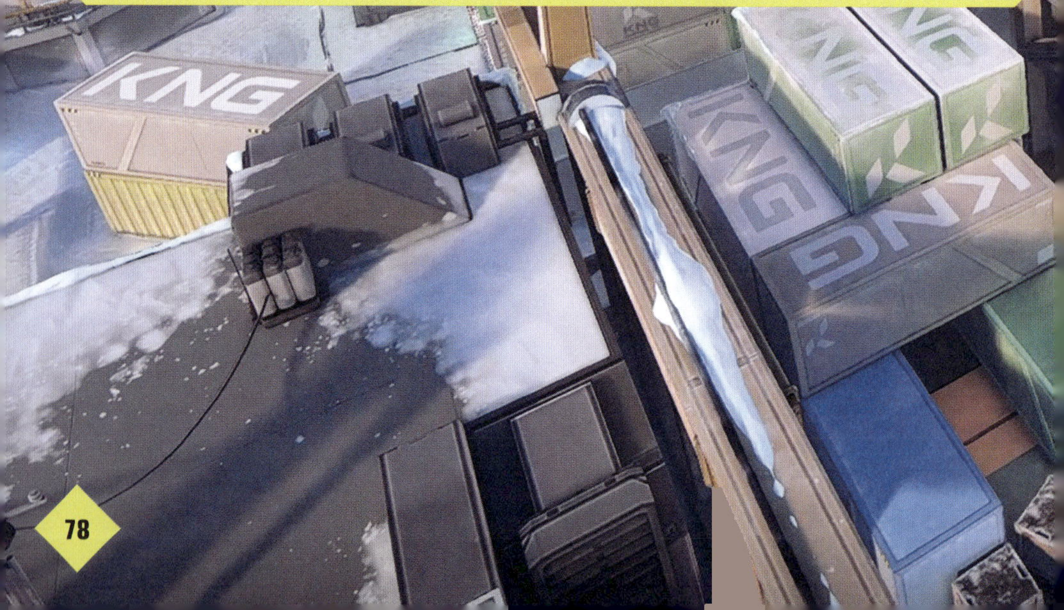

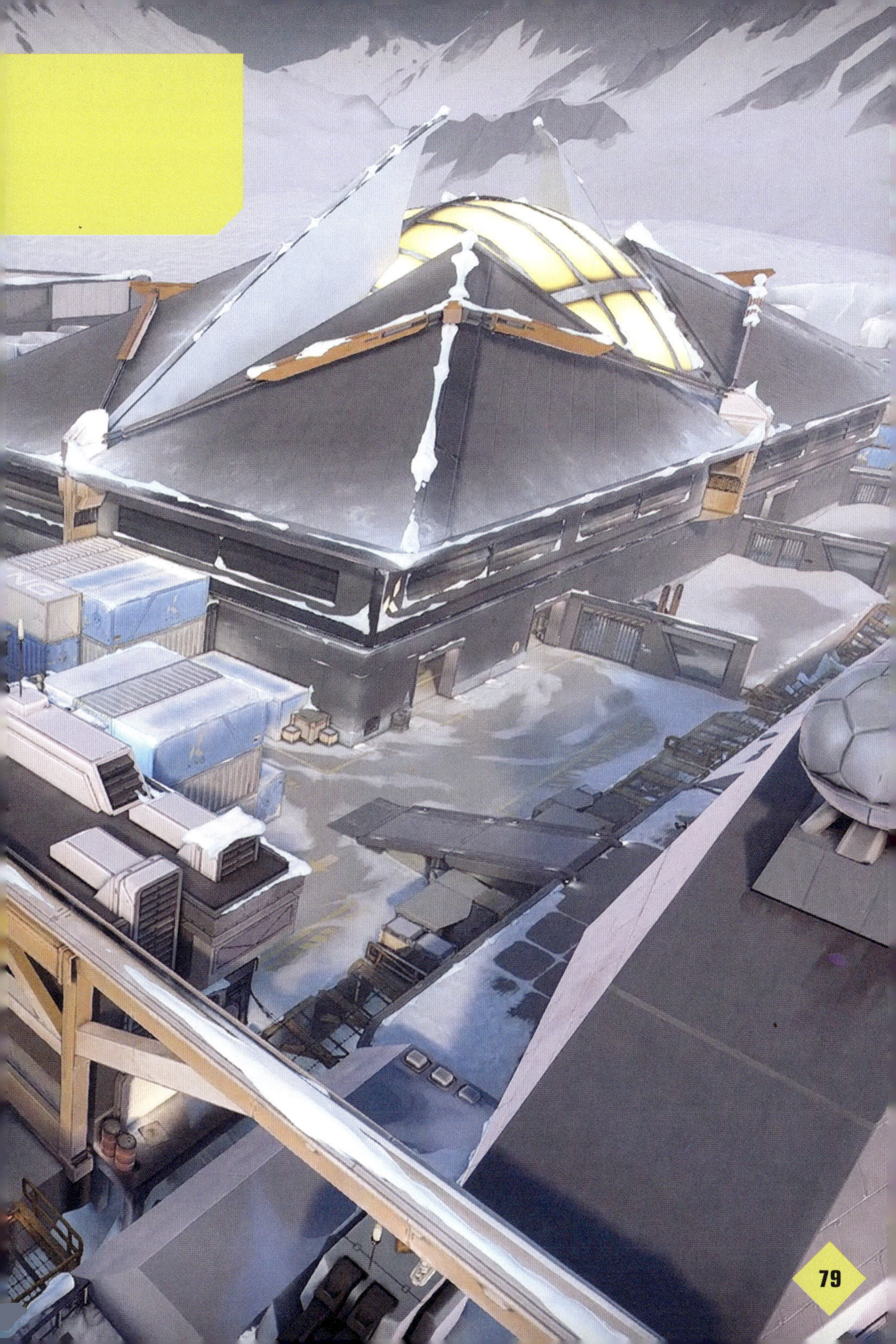

ONLINE SAFETY INFORMATION

YOUNGER FANS' GUIDE

Spending time online with others is great fun. As Valorant might be your first experience of digital socialising, here are a few simple rules to help you stay safe and keep the internet an awesome place to spend time:

• Never give out your real name – don't use it as your username.
• Never give out any of your personal details.
• Never tell anybody which school you go to or how old you are.
• Before playing Valorant, ask a parent or guardian for permission.
• Take regular breaks, as well as playing with parents nearby, or in shared family rooms.
• Always tell a parent or guardian if something is worrying you.

PARENTS' GUIDE

Sound

Sound is crucial in Valorant – players will often wear headphones to hear every noise, which means parents won't be able to hear what is being said by strangers. It's possible to set up sound to come through a computer's speakers via the Sound section of the Settings menu so you can hear everything being said.

Online Chat

In Valorant, there is live onscreen text chat between users, and live voice chat from your team. You can turn off Team Voice Chat in Settings, but not text chat. However, you can mute individual players from the pause menu within games to stop messages appearing in chat and also stop their voice communications.

Screen Time

Taking regular breaks is important. Set play sessions by using a timer. Some games can last over half an hour and if your child leaves in the middle of the round, they could leave their team short of a person and receive an in-game ban. It is advisable to give an advanced warning for stopping play or clearly outlining a stopping point before play begins.

Reporting Players

If a player is being abusive in an online game, you can report them from the pause menu, or after a game has ended. Press Esc to access the pause menu, then the Report button by the player that you want to report. You can do the same thing from the Scoreboard tab in Career after a match has ended.

In-Game Purchases

Valorant does offer the ability for players to make in-game purchases for items such as new weapon skins, also known as Cosmetics. They're not required to play the game and they don't improve a player's performance.

There are two different currencies in Valorant, Radianite Points and Valorant Points, both of which can be purchased with real-world money and are used for different purposes. It is possible to earn Valorant Points by completing the free battle pass.

The battle pass has free and paid tiers. The paid tier has rewards at every level a player passes during a season, whereas the free one only has intermittent rewards. All rewards are still cosmetic and don't affect how the game is played.

PEGI Rating

In the UK, guidance ratings are supplied by PEGI (Pan European Game Information). Valorant is rated as PEGI 16. Parents should be aware of the recommended age set by their local advisory board and decide whether their children should play.